Global Corporate Strategy and Trade Policy

International business today functions in an environment increasingly dominated by the 'triad' of economic power formed by the USA, Japan and the European Community. Multinational corporate strategies have to be formulated within the context of intense global competition between these three economic blocs.

Alan Rugman and Alain Verbeke analyse the interplay between the trade policies adopted by the major powers and the competitive strategies of international corporations. For businesses located in small open economies it is of paramount importance to secure access to the market of at least one of the triad powers. This reality forms a major determinant of corporate strategic management among firms engaged in international competition.

With particular reference to trade relations between Canada and the USA, the effects of Japanese multinational dominance and the implications of European economic integration, this volume throws new light on the interaction between international business and government trade policies. It will be essential reading for students of international trade and business, corporate strategy and global management.

ALAN RUGMAN is Professor of International Business at the University of Toronto, and Research Director of the Ontario Centre for International Business. He has written and edited many books on international business and management, including *Multinationals and Canada–United States Free Trade* (1990). He is series editor for the Routledge International Business series.

ALAIN VERBEKE is Visiting Professor in the Faculty of Management at the University of Toronto. He also holds academic appointments at the University of Antwerp and Brussels University. He is the author of numerous refereed articles on business policy and international business strategy.

International Business Series
Academic Editor: Alan M. Rugman, University of Toronto

Global Corporate Strategy and Trade Policy

Alan Rugman and Alain Verbeke

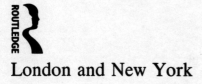

London and New York

First published by Routledge 1990
11 New Fetter Lane, London EC4P 4EE

Simultaneously published in the USA and Canada
by Routledge
a division of Routledge, Chapman and Hall, Inc.
29 West 35th Street, New York, NY 10001

British Library Cataloguing in Publication Data

Rugman, Alan M.
  Global corporate strategy and trade policy
  1. Multinational companies. Corporate planning. Effect of
  government policies on foreign trade. Foreign trade.
  Policies of governments. Effects on corporate planning of
  multinational companies
  I. Title II. Verbeke, Alain
  658.4012

  ISBN 0–415–05195–9

Library of Congress Cataloging-in-Publication Data

Rugman, Alan M.
  Global corporate strategy and trade policy / Alan Rugman and
  Alain Verbeke.
      p.   cm. — (International business series)
  Includes bibliographical references and index.
  ISBN 0–415–05195–9
  1. International business enterprises—Management. 2. Strategic
  planning. 3. Commercial policy. I. Verbeke, Alain. II. Title
  III. Series: International business series (London, England)
  HD62.4.R84   1990
  658.4′012—dc20   90–43471
                                                              CIP

Printed and bound in Great Britain by
Biddles Ltd, Guildford and King's Lynn

Contents

Contents

Figures

Tables

Acknowledgements

The authors are pleased to acknowledge the financial support for their work on this topic by the Research Programme, Ontario Centre for International Business, based at the Faculty of Management of the University of Toronto. In addition, Professor Rugman received valuable support while serving as Royal Bank Visiting Professor of International Business at the University of Alberta in 1988.

Helpful comments have been provided by numerous colleagues in the field of international business. In particular, this book has been stimulated by help from Jean Boddewyn of the City University of New York, Mark Casson of the University of Reading, John Dunning of the University of Reading, Stefanie Lenway of the University of Minnesota, David Rutenberg of Queens University and Robert Sexty of Memorial University.

The authors have received first-class research assistance from Thomas Boddez. They also acknowledge with thanks the excellent secretarial support on this project by Amy Ho.

Chapter one

Introduction

The focus of this book is the interaction between government trade policy and corporate strategy within a global trading environment. The relationship between the formulation and implementation of trade policy and corporate strategy will be analysed. To provide a realistic perspective, the Canada–US Free Trade Agreement and other examples relevant to small, open trading economies, will be utilized. These serve to illustrate the realities of doing business in our integrated but regulated global trading system. We will extend our discussion of trade policy to include the economics-related issues of industrial policy in general. These will be examined from both a management and a public-policy perspective.

Triad power and corporate strategy

Several management scholars have discussed the increasing importance of global competition.[1] Of particular interest are the triad powers, which account for the vast majority of global trade and investment. The largest 500 multinational enterprises (MNEs) are mainly from the triad economies, and account for well over half of all the world's trade.[2] Triad power has been identified as a major environmental determinant of corporate strategic management by Ohmae (1985). He has argued that the traditional view of the world economy being dominated by the United States should be replaced by a more realistic perspective which recognizes the existence of triad power, i.e. intense global competition between the firms of three economic blocs: the United States, Japan and the European Community.

For businesses located in small open economies, like Canada, which do not form a part of the triad, it is of paramount importance to secure access to the market of at least one of the triad powers. This is essential for the long-term survival, profitability and growth of the corporation and thus for the nation. In a world characterized by increasing protectionism it is vital for non-triad corporations to have access for their trade and investment to a triad market.

Yet US corporations have a new weapon to deny market access to foreign rivals. A key theme of this book is that US business planners may be acting in a rational manner (from the standpoint of their own self-interest) when they put pressure on government to erect barriers to import competition. But their action subverts trade laws that had been designed to serve the nation as a whole. Such action also does not work. It provides only temporary relief to companies and domestic industries that come to rely on government to shelter them from foreign competition.[3]

The view taken in this book is that all companies should normally aim to obtain competitive advantages by pursuing an efficiency-based strategy. US producers have traditionally been successful in maintaining their competitive ability. Yet many of them now appear to be turning away from the economic base of their success. They are becoming reliant on government action to put barriers in the way of imports.

Companies whose survival, profits or growth have been endangered by their failures on economic grounds often stop trying to pursue a strategy of low cost or uniqueness of products and services. A common tactic in this situation is to head to the seats of political power and argue for government protection in order to maintain employment and output in the face of 'unfair' (subsidized) foreign competition.

Most industrial countries now have enacted more rigorous anti-dumping and countervailing duty trade remedy laws following adoption in 1979 of the Subsidies Code under the General Agreement on Tariffs and Trade (GATT). Such procedures are generally acknowledged to be necessary to enforce fair trading practices. However, a number of US producers are using the trade remedy laws to obtain shelter from international competition.

Corporate strategists, through their active lobbying and interaction with government bureaucrats and politicians, have found ways to turn the political process to their own advantage. In this manner, trade policy moves from the pursuit of national goals towards a more commercial and self-serving set of competitive entry barriers.

Obviously, the best triad partner for Canada is its closest geographical neighbour, the United States. In this book, the view is taken that trade liberalization between Canada and the United States is the most efficient way for Canadian firms to circumvent

US-administered protection. It remains necessary for Canada to work through multilateral trade forums to induce greater accord with the principles of trade liberalization. This multilateral route should not, however, ignore the urgent necessity of a bilateral trading arrangement with the United States.

Corporate strategy and trade policy

Another theme in this book is the close degree of interaction between business and government. In the formulation of trade and industrial policy, these two groups interact to an unprecedented degree. In terms of the formulation of industrial policy in general, and trade policy in particular, the private sector is now often a lead player. In some cases, as during the 1979 GATT round[4] and the 1986–8 period of the Canada–US free trade negotiations, the private sector is also a partner in the process of public-policy formulation.[5]

In business schools today the analysis of environmental factors, including international ones, is a regular component of the curriculum in strategic management. In most well-organized triad-based corporations involved in trade and investment activities with each other, the precepts of global strategic management are used with an increasing degree of sophistication and relevance. Canadian-based MNEs have also taken on board these modern techniques.[6] The result is a keener analysis of the interactive nature of business–government relations, especially in the international dimension.

The involvement of business with the various layers of government in the United States is probably even greater than in Canada, while the active partnership of the state and business in post-war Japanese economic development is already legendary. The picture is more complicated in Europe due to the mélange of nations involved in the European Community, but the role of the state in international business activity is certainly important. Thus Canadian government and business, in dealing with the triad, must recognize these interdependencies. They need to work together to formulate policies which will promote Canadian economic prosperity through commercial progress.

Structure of the book

The second chapter considers corporate strategy and its relationship to government policy in general. A new framework (visualized through the use of a 2 × 2 matrix of corporate strategies) is introduced that distinguishes between two generic types of corporate strategies. These are efficiency-based strategies and non-efficiency-based strategies. The way in which these two types of corporate strategies are related to government policy, especially trade policy, is then analysed, again using a new matrix. The findings on policy implementation are generalizable to public issues other than trade policy. For example, the impact of corporate behaviour on subsidies for research and development (R&D), selective financial grants and other elements of industrial policy, is similar to its impact on trade policy.

Chapter 3 focuses on the primary topic of this book: trade policy. It will demonstrate, again through the use of a new matrix framework, how the 'technical track' of US trade remedy law investigations has become politicized and subject to influence by corporations seeking shelter from foreign rivals. The result is a form of 'administered' protection. This framework of trade policy objectives and instruments provides us with a new type of competitive strategy whereby shelter can be obtained by corporations if they lobby trade regulatory agencies. While this is currently a particularly US phenomenon we believe that this process will be adopted in many other countries, leading to a new type of corporate-led protectionism. We illustrate this problem through an investigation of the bilateral Free Trade Agreement between Canada and the United States, which came into force on 1 January 1989.

Chapter 4 extends the corporate strategy aspects of the new framework developed in the first two chapters. In particular, a new analysis is developed of the strategic alternatives available to Canadian managers faced with the non-efficiency-based strategies of US firms and the attendant increased US protectionism. These new conceptual ideas are then linked to the actual strategic behaviour of Canadian firms during the trade negotiations between Canada and the United States in the 1986–8 period. It is observed that the future survival of large Canadian companies in an integrated North American and interdependent global economy depends upon a thorough understanding of the linkages between public policy and corporate strategy.

Chapter 5 takes the Canada–US Free Trade Agreement as a specific example of environmental changes in trade and investment policy. We evaluate the methods by which Canadian-based corporations will adjust to the new trading environment. We examine the competitive strategies of two sets of multinational enterprises: first, those of Canadian-owned multinationals and, second, those of the subsidiaries of US multinationals in Canada. Throughout the analysis we consider the ways in which corporate strategies are influenced both by global trading patterns and by the changes in the more local bilateral trading arrangements.

Chapter 6 extends our model of the interaction between corporate strategies and government policies, especially trade policies, to a broader framework. In particular, the corporate strategies of corporations in the 'triad' economies of Japan, Europe and America are considered as are the trade policies of these blocs. This involves an extension of the public policy part of the new framework proposed earlier and the inclusion of more complex real-world examples, related to Japan and the European Community. This involves a series of linked 2 × 2 matrices which are developed in a sequential manner to provide insights into dynamic behaviour.

In summarizing the first half of the book, the point needs to be made that the Canada–US Free Trade Agreement and the Canadian experience with US-administered protection is a representative example of changing global trends. Both trade and investment policies are being reconsidered as the Japanese success in using an industrial policy becomes more apparent to Western nations. Other developments in the global trading system are also affecting corporate strategy. The European Community is speeding up its development of an integrated single market for 1992, the GATT is working to develop broader coverage of services and non-tariff barriers to trade, while the newly industrialized countries (NICs) are performing well in a world of triad power. The manner in which corporations from these various economies can use trade and industrial policies to their advantage is a global question of great interest. It is particularly relevant for managers since their future survival in an integrated and interdependent global economy depends upon such an understanding.

Chapter 7 relates the completed analytical framework of corporate strategy to current and future options for both public policy makers and corporate strategic planners. The way in which globalization and nationally responsive strategies need to be modelled together is applied to the investment and trade policy implications of the Canada–US Free Trade Agreement. Of particular interest are innovations such as the application of national treatment to services and the binational trade law review panels, both of which are examples of the trade-offs involved in today's globally integrated yet nationalistic world. Such dual policy initiatives are already causing public officials and corporate planners to revise their attitudes towards corporate strategy and trade policy. This, in turn, leads to changes in the nature of strategic management and policy implementation.

In Chapter 8 we consider the issue of an optimal industrial policy for a small open economy. The different options available to Canadian public policy makers are examined and related to the earlier analysis. It is found that an industrial policy of 'selective differentiation' is the only viable option available to small open economies like Canada. This allows such nations to retain secure access to large markets and, at the same time, foster the future international competitiveness of domestic industries.

Finally, in Chapter 9 our thinking about industrial policy is applied to the real world example of the recent report of the Premier's Council of Ontario. We consider whether or not policies to support industries on a selective and discriminatory basis are viable. The Premier's Council study is somewhat similar to plans drawn up for other sub-national units and small open economies, so our analysis is relevant on a broader basis.

Chapter two

Corporate strategic management

Introduction

In this chapter a new framework is developed to analyse and assess strategies of firms towards their environment, especially government regulation. Four basic options are available to strategic planners as guiding mechanisms for firm behaviour. The nature of the strategies developed and the channels used to pursue them are analysed in relation to government trade policies. Emphasis is put on the interactions between firms seeking protectionism and government. It is shown that firms can obtain unintended trade policy outputs by influencing the process of government policy making. In this case objectives related to national economic efficiency may well be subverted and government agencies are stimulated to pursue distribution objectives. If firms are able to influence trade policy in this way, high costs are imposed on society at large as shelter from international competition invariably diminishes consumer welfare in the long run.

At the frontier between economics, political science and management, there is a new business literature being developed which addresses the issue of how a firm interacts with government policy makers. This literature has its roots in the industrial organization side of economics, the area of conflict resolution and lobbying activities in political science and the concepts of strategic planning in management. The ideas from this literature have a useful application in the world of international business, particularly in the case of trade policy.

Critical in this new literature is analysis of the manner in which the strategic planners of the firm react to environmental changes, such as new directions in government policy. Michael Porter, of the Harvard Business School, has developed a paradigm of three generic strategies which capture the essentials of the firm's competitive strategies (Porter 1980, 1985). These strategies are: cost

7

competition, product differentiation, and focus. All of these are basically efficiency-based strategies subject to environmental constraints such as government policy, which are beyond the firm's control. In this chapter we extend these principles of strategic management and apply them to the issue of trade policy.[1] In Chapter 5, the Porter framework will be used again as a basis for predicting the likely responses of business firms to free trade.

Corporate strategic management and trade policy

The major contribution in this chapter is our focus upon the interactive nature of corporate strategic management and trade policy formulation. Corporate strategic management is defined here as all patterns in decisions and actions, aimed at improving or maintaining the firm's survival, profitability and growth. In this context, it is of paramount importance to recognize that strategic planners of firms not only react to trade policy measures as environmental constraints but actively lobby and interact with government bureaucrats and politicians as a means of using the political process to their own advantage. This process serves to give some firms a competitive advantage *vis-à-vis* foreign rivals. The problem here is that two types of competitive advantages resulting from government regulation should be distinguished. First, some trade policy measures may improve the firm's ability to provide cheaper or unique products to its customers. In this case, trade policy measures build upon the firm-specific advantages (FSAs) of the company involved. In other words trade policy measures complement the firm's skills at achieving low costs or differentiating its products.

Second, other trade policy measures merely impose artificial costs on foreign competitors, without improving the sheltered firm's strengths in the areas of cost reduction or differentiation; examples include barriers to trade such as tariffs and non-tariff barriers. However, due to the nature of such barriers to trade (which, if maintained indefinitely, protect uncompetitive firms and industries at the expense of consumers and the long-run national interest), there is a problem facing the strategic planners of the firm. Their short-run success at achieving shelter by protection usually results in the perpetuation or development of inefficiencies which can erode the long-run competitive edge of the firm. In other words, government trade policy becomes a substitute instead of a complement for the company's FSAs.[2]

If two types of government trade policy measures can be distinguished, this implies that firms can pursue two different types of strategic activities to influence government policy: first, strategic activities that improve or at least build upon the firm's ability to achieve low costs or differentiate its products; and second, strategic activities aimed at creating shelter, i.e. trade policy measures which artificially protect the firm from its international market environment. The former will be depicted here as efficiency-based strategies, the latter as non-efficiency-based strategies. We define efficiency-based strategies as all decisions and actions that aim at achieving survival, profit and growth through the provision of products and services to the firm's customers that are cheaper than or differentiated from those of potential competitors. The competitive strengths of the firm then primarily flow from FSAs or natural country-specific advantages or both,[3] merely complemented by government measures.

Non-efficiency-based strategies can be defined as all decisions and actions aimed at achieving survival, profit and growth or any other set of economic objectives through means other than the provision of cheaper or better products and services to the firm's customers as compared with competitors. A non-efficiency-based strategy shelters the firm from competitive pressures; one method being through the development of strategies to secure trade barriers against rival (foreign) companies. Another method is by forming a cartel, a form of 'natural' shelter, in contrast to trade protection.[4] A firm could even seek to eliminate competition altogether, by obtaining a monopoly from government.

Another possibility is that a set of objectives other than survival, profit and growth is being pursued. Examples include company compliance with public-policy objectives of maintaining high (inefficient) employment levels; sustaining declining industries; and increasing income levels in underdeveloped regions. In such cases the achievement of low costs or uniqueness of the products and services provided may be unimportant for the firms involved.

It could of course be argued, when using a profit maximization point of view, that all firms will develop both efficiency- and non-efficiency-based activities up to the point where the marginal costs of both types of activities equal their marginal benefits (a view defended by economists who have studied so-called rent-seeking activities by business firms, i.e. activities through which resources are devoted to obtain wealth from society instead of creating wealth). In reality, the costs for a firm resulting from non-efficiency-based activities are not necessarily always related to their benefits. There are two main reasons for this.

First, some types of shelter, such as the complete elimination of foreign imports in the domestic market, may require low costs.

This occurs where government is very sensitive to the demands of the firm seeking shelter. In addition, if such shelter becomes institutionalized in laws or regulations without being restricted in time, costs may be very low for firms in order to maintain existing levels of protection. In more general terms, it could be stated that the supply of shelter is often unrelated to the costs incurred by the firms demanding shelter.

Second, many firms may refuse to engage in non-efficiency-based strategies because these are in contradiction with the still dominating view in market economies that 'fair' competition based on FSAs and natural country-specific advantages should be the basis of any firm's survival, profitability and growth. Hence, a 'Darwinian' approach is used in this book: in general, firms will only seek shelter when they cannot compete on the basis of cost or differentiation advantages (this issue is discussed further on p. 14).

The question still arises of whether firms will develop strategic policies individually or collectively (for example by promoting some industry-wide position). This is not an important issue: firms which need shelter will attempt to gain shelter. If other firms in the industry have similar needs, collective action may be taken depending upon industry structure. If preferences towards the creation of shelter strongly differ in the industry, this may prevent industry-wide collective action.[5]

The strategic planners can use two 'channels' to implement their chosen strategies, positioning the firm in either its market environment (coping with market forces) or its non-market environment (coping with non-market forces). The non-market environment consists of government(s) as regulator(s) and pressure groups.

Recognizing these disparate strategies available to strategic planners of firms and the channels used to achieve them, four basic options can be distinguished, in the respective cells of Figure 2.1. In other words, this matrix allows us to classify all strategic actions and decisions made by a firm into four categories.

The four options for strategic planners

Option 1 The strategic planners can opt to pursue efficiency-based strategies by positioning the firm in its market environment. Economic theory describes and analyses such behaviour.[6] In this case actions are developed to cope with, for example, competitors, providers of inputs and buyers of outputs. Porter's cost–leadership is a self-evident example of an efficiency-based strategy, as are the differentiation and focus strategies.

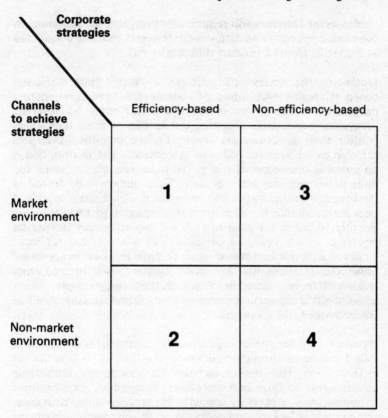

Figure 2.1 The corporate strategy matrix

Option 2: The firm's policy makers can still pursue cost or differentiation strategies, but they emphasize the issue of coping with non-market forces.[7] Such firms have to comply with, or are influenced by, government regulation and intervention. Firms may also be involved in bargaining with governments, or in exercising corporate social responsibility to merge private sector economic objectives into public sector social and political values.

It is self-evident that options 1 and 2 go together well, and it will depend on the characteristics of the firm's activities which option will dominate. For example, if nearly all sales are made to government-controlled customers, as is sometimes the case with aircraft, telecommunications equipment and electrical power systems, the second option may be extremely important for the firms involved. Similarly, government procurement, defence and other

11

public sector activities will require that firms operate according to the second option; to an extent such strategies could be considered as a specific form of product differentiation.

Option 3 The strategic planners can be pursuing non-efficiency-based strategies even when positioning the firm in its market environment. The choice of this option can often be observed in declining industries, whereby the inefficient firms themselves (rather than governments) try to limit competitive pressures through cartel or other collusive agreements. The third option is an unstable one, especially in global industries where cartels and monopolies are inevitably eroded. Thus, they will be forced in the long run to shift to the first option or to exit. Exits may indeed become inevitable because firms that attempt to remain in the third quadrant in the long run often completely cease to pursue strategies of low cost and uniqueness of products and services.[8] In practice, it is sometimes difficult to distinguish efficiency-based behaviour (for example low cost objective, first option) from behaviour merely aimed at closing markets (for example elimination of efficiency-seeking competitors by firms engaging in collusive behaviour, third option).

Option 4 Finally, the strategic planners can pursue non-efficiency-based strategies through positioning the firm in its non-market environment. This option includes requesting and influencing governments to raise barriers against competition or to receive subsidies, reduce taxes or confer other such advantages to compensate for a lack of cost-reducing or differentiation-enhancing potential. Examples would be attempts to seek tariff or non-tariff protection and public subsidies for sunset industries.[9] It is clear that this option, as well as the third option, invariably diminishes national economic welfare if pursued in the long run. We should recognize, however, that temporary shelter may sometimes give 'breathing space' to firms faced with unexpected environmental changes that threaten their survival (for example sudden changes in exchange rates). In this case the third as well as the fourth strategy, although substituting for strong FSAs, may be viable alternatives for the sheltered firms in the short run. Moreover, even national economic efficiency may be served in this case, especially if the firms with shelter possess substantial assets that cannot be easily redeployed elsewhere in the economy.

In practical situations, problems also may arise when trying to make a distinction between the second and fourth option. There are a number of situations whereby firms pursuing efficiency-based strategies may interact with governments, thus creating entry barriers for foreign competitors. Such government intervention may include: the allocation of subsidies and special tax concessions and other advantages to multinationals that set up a subsidiary in a host country; the provision of health and welfare services which help raise the value of human capital; public insurance for business transactions; the use of diplomatic representation in foreign countries for purposes of export promotion; and the use of special public assistance development and infrastructure projects. All of these events can result in a higher entry barrier benefiting the firm but not really substituting for its FSAs. In contrast, the fourth option is designed to shelter the firm through government intervention and protection. This process serves to generate artificial costs for competitors without doing anything to improve substantially the ability of the protected firm to achieve lower costs or differentiate its products.[10]

Once a firm engages in the second or fourth option it becomes important to influence trade policy, as it determines to a large extent the firm's competitive advantages *vis-à-vis* foreign rivals. In both cases active strategic behaviour may lead to the creation of trade barriers. The second option would then include, for example, certain export-promoting measures, such as export subsidies, which would facilitate a firm's ability to penetrate foreign markets. In contrast, the fourth option would refer to trade barriers aimed at being a substitute for the firm's skills in achieving low costs and differentiating products. A special case would be the infant industry and old industry arguments for protecting the domestic market. Here government protection is clearly a form of shelter from foreign competition in the short run, but if domestic competition is maintained this could lead to the creation of strong FSAs by domestic firms. In other words, the firms involved would have a long-term primary strategy located in quadrant 1 of Figure 2.1, but at the same time protection against foreign rivals (resulting from a quadrant 4 strategy) would be a short-term secondary strategy.

Recent research on the behaviour of business during the trade negotiations between Canada and the United States in 1986–7 demonstrates the relevance of the conceptual framework developed above.[11] The majority of large businesses are pursuing primary strategies in quadrant 1 of Figure 2.1. These include large Canadian multinationals, such as Northern Telecom, Alcan and Noranda, but also most large foreign-owned subsidiaries, such as

Ford of Canada, General Motors of Canada, General Electric Canada and Du Pont Canada.

Although these successful multinationals pursue quadrant 1 strategies, when these firms have attempted to influence government they are positioning themselves in quadrant 2, as will be demonstrated in Chapters 4 and 5. These firms are already well prepared to compete in a global environment. This is as a result of extensive recent rationalizations to obtain new cost and differentiation advantages. Hence these corporations do not need shelter, but rather an institutional environment that will allow them to compete on the basis of their FSAs. In contrast, it is clear that other Canadian firms such as Labatt, which rely on government shelter, and food-processing firms protected by agricultural marketing boards, have lobbied to remain exempt from any possible free trade. These firms are positioning themselves in the fourth quadrant.

Why non-efficiency-based strategies fail

In order to assess the impact of efficiency- and non-efficiency-based strategies on the competitive position of firms in the long run, a distinction needs to be made between companies with strong FSAs and those with weak FSAs. A strong FSA is defined here as a company-based skill or know-how which is potentially sufficient to ensure competitiveness *vis-à-vis* foreign rivals, while a weak FSA is, by itself, insufficient to allow competitiveness and profitability in the international marketplace.

Four different cases of corporate trade policy strategies can then be distinguished, as represented in Figure 2.2. Here the horizontal axis identifies the strategy of the firm and the vertical axis measures the strength of its FSAs.

The first quadrant represents the case whereby firms with strong firm-specific advantages pursue an efficiency-based strategy towards trade policy. The main objective of these firms, when trying to influence government policy, is to decrease their own costs or to enhance their differentiation capability when operating in the international environment. An active government trade policy, including export subsidies, may complement a corporate efficiency strategy. It may generate spill-over effects from one sector to the rest of the economy as well as profit-shifting effects, on an international scale, in which case potential foreign rivals may not enter the market. Such subsidies do not necessarily shelter a firm from foreign competition, but may improve its competitive position.

14

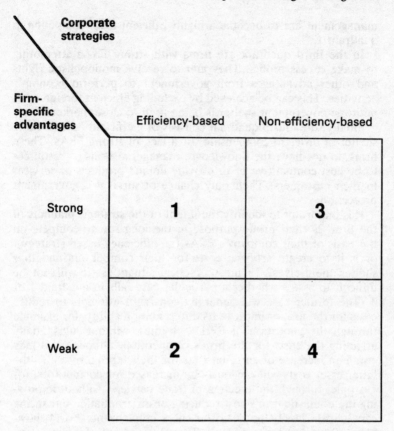

Figure 2.2 Corporate trade policy strategies

In the second quadrant are firms in infant industries. These industries and firms facing temporary difficulties are not able to compete on an international scale in the short run because of weak FSAs. They may become internationally competitive in the long run, if helped by government, normally through the imposition of entry barriers or the allocation of resources to the infant industry, or both. Government-imposed entry barriers may involve the allocation of resources to R&D, production or marketing activities of the firm, or the erection of tariff and non-tariff barriers against foreign rivals. Although such behaviour should be interpreted as a quadrant 4 strategy in the short run, this may only be a secondary option if the long-term aims of the firm's management are to become a highly efficient firm, competing in quadrant 1.

In the third quadrant are firms with strong FSAs attempting to make excess profits. They aim to receive monopolistic rights and other advantages from government to perform economic activities. This can be achieved by excluding efficient foreign competitors; government shelter is being used to close markets.

Finally, the fourth quadrant consists of inefficient firms seeking shelter in order to compensate for a lack of strong FSAs. These firms do not have the knowledge, managerial skills or resources to be cost competitive or to provide unique products or services to their customers. Their only chance of survival is government protection.

It is important to identify the intent of the strategic planners of the firm. Is their prime purpose in the long run to compete on the basis of their company's FSAs (an efficiency-based strategy), or is it to create artificial costs for their competitors and thus shelter themselves? In most practical situations, it will not be difficult to assess whether a particular case falls in quadrant 1 or 3. The former case will generally consist of attempts to reduce costs for the firm or improve its differentation ability, for example through the allocation of R&D subsidies, without substantially affecting the costs for the firm's competition, although this may entail an increase of entry barriers for their foreign rivals. In the latter case, costs will obviously be increased for competitors, for example, through the erection of trade barriers, without improving the domestic firm's cost-reducing or differentiation-enhancing capability. Classifying particular cases in quadrants 2 or 4, however, may prove more difficult. The development of infant industries, or the procurement of temporary relief to declining industries, may require the creation of trade barriers in the short run (and hence a temporary increase in costs for efficient foreign rivals), although the protected companies may actually pursue a long-run efficiency-based strategy.

It is our contention, however, that firms seeking the erection of trade barriers are in any case pursuing non-efficiency-based strategies and should be placed in quadrant 4, in spite of 'infant industry' or 'temporary relief' arguments. An infant industry protection policy can then only succeed in the case of active domestic competition, which allows the development of winners and the weeding out of losers. In this case, the firms involved pay more attention to domestic efficiency-based strategies than to the creation of shelter from foreign rivals. Moreover, such government policies will only be successful if they are self-liquidating.[12]

When the old industry argument is used as a rationale to intro-
duce trade protectionism, a long-run efficiency-based strategy
would exist only if the intent of the corporate managers is to use
the adjustment programmes on a temporary basis, for example
for a period up to ten years, in order to regain international
competitiveness without government support.[13] Unfortunately,
this argument is often used in cases where country-specific advantages are weak in a structural sense (for example because of high
labour costs in a labour-intensive industry) or where structural
shifts in the industry have reduced future profit potential for
domestic suppliers (such as when excess capacity exists on a global
scale). In these cases the intent of corporate management may be
to gain indefinite shelter or to use the rents achieved through
protectionism to diversify into other, more profitable activities.
Structural characteristics of the domestic global industry may
make it impossible for domestic suppliers to become internationally competitive again. In this case, more direct measures
than trade protectionism may be more efficient in permitting an
orderly contraction of the domestic segment of the industry, taking
into account the issue of labour adjustment.

An example of the misuse of the argument for temporary
breathing space is provided by the US integrated steel producers
who have attempted to secure several types of shelter against
imports since 1969.[14] In terms of policy formulation, US trade
protectionism was explicitly aimed at restoring international competitiveness in the domestic steel industry, through new investments and restructuring efforts. In practice, the main result has,
by the creation of shelter, allowed the steel firms involved to
diversify through acquisitions and to limit reductions of employment in this high-wage industry.

A related point is that quadrant 2 is an unstable one. In the
long run, firms that have developed strong FSAs will shift from
quadrant 2 to quadrant 1, while firms that have been unsuccessful
in generating strong FSAs will move to quadrant 4, in order to
secure survival. Quadrant 3 is also an unstable quadrant in the
case of global industries, as highly efficient firms do not need to
rely on trade barriers. This implies a shift to the first quadrant.
In contrast, even highly efficient firms may see their FSAs being
eroded in the long run. This occurs when there is an excessive
reliance on government protection. This causes the firm to move
to the fourth quadrant.

Conclusion

It has been demonstrated here that strategic management in firms interacts strongly with government policy, especially in the international business area. It is our contention that any analysis of corporate strategic management and government activities should make a distinction between behaviour guided by efficiency-based objectives and that guided by non-efficiency-based objectives. Influencing trade policy is an extremely important strategy for firms. It helps to determine their competitive position relative to foreign rivals operating in an international environment.

Distinguishing efficiency- from non-efficiency-based behaviour is crucial. The efficiency-based strategy attempts to use trade policy as a complement to the company's FSA. In contrast, the non-efficiency-based strategy will lead to shelter, i.e. trade policy measures which substitute for strong FSAs. In other words, the 'fourth option' basically allows the survival and profitability of firms that cannot compete on the basis of low costs or differentiated products. From the point of view of the strategic planners of a firm, the fourth option is a rational short-term action alternative. Yet, when used as the firm's primary strategy, in the long run no ability is retained to compete on the basis of costs or product differentiation.

Chapter three

Trade policy and corporate strategy

The relevance of trade policy to corporate strategies

We will demonstrate in this chapter that today the strategic planners of American corporations can use a new type of competitive strategy against foreign rivals. In addition to general protectionist measures and other regulations on importers, they have politicized the US trade law investigations. Some Canadian firms also follow this political strategy, but it is less of an issue for the global economy due to the small size of the Canadian market compared to other members of the triad. Aimed mainly at the Japanese and Europeans, US protectionism really hurts its largest trading partner, Canada. To demonstrate the interactive nature of US corporate strategy and US protectionism, the framework developed in Chapter 1 is applied using cases involving resource products traded between Canada and the United States.

It is shown how American corporations use US trade remedy law actions and other legal trade measures, all of which require investigations, leading to harassment and costs to foreign firms. Public policy is shown to be a device through which US corporations can change the costs of operating in the United States that are faced by different competitors. It is important for academic economists to recognize that policy measures such as changes in trade barriers are not merely exogenous factors, but are really variables that firms can influence.

Trade policy formulation

The trade policy objectives of government are broad and may include both efficiency-based and distributional (or non-efficiency-based) objectives. The former are concerned with creating and maintaining national wealth attributes which have so far been the focus of the discussion (albeit including here the issue of

19

externalities). Non-efficiency-based objectives relate to the distribution of wealth and to the government's provision of defence and security; cultural and political autonomy; social programmes; and related aspects of sovereignty. It could be argued that a third set of objectives, aimed at achieving macro-economic stabilization (for example in terms of employment or prices) should be distinguished. The evolution of several macro-economic indicators may obviously be influenced by trade policy measures. However, in our view most concrete trade policy measures aimed at achieving stabilization are either primarily efficiency- or equity-based, in terms of both the intent of the relevant public policy makers and the outputs of the trade policy measures.

National trade policy objectives (trade policy formulation) can be identified by analysing policy documents and policy statements. Regardless of the objectives pursued, two structural instruments can be used to carry out trade policy, namely a political track, which is directly and formally accountable to political constituencies, and a technical track (or bureaucracy).[1] A technical track is important when public policy makers wish to have efficiency-based objectives pursued by public agencies not subject to political pressures. It is then assumed that the legislative authorities act as a broker for various regional and sectoral interests, generating trade laws which are in the national interest, and then allow a technical track to use efficiency-based criteria and legal procedures to implement such a policy. Only if trade law formulation can be removed from political lobbying does it make sense to have a technical track, using economics-based criteria and legal procedures to implement such a policy.[2]

A problem, however, is that the public choice literature in economics suggests that politicians act out of self-interest, for example to maximize the probabilities of being re-elected.[3] This calls into question the basic integrity of a brokerage function by the political system, and the ability of the technical track to administer laws and procedures without becoming subject to outside influences. These problems will be returned to after the distinction between the political track and a workable technical track is made.

Four options are available to government when formulating trade policy. These require choosing between efficiency or distributional objectives and choosing the structural instruments to attain these objectives. These four options are represented in Figure 3.1. All trade policy activities carried out by government can then be classified into the four quadrants of this figure.

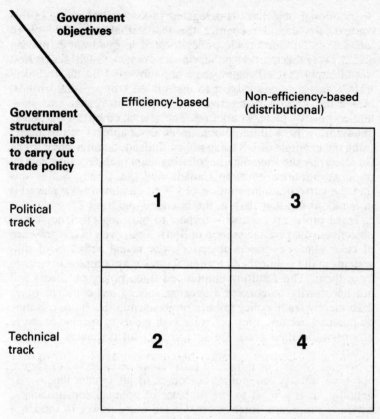

Figure 3.1 Formulation of trade policy

Option 1 includes the classic free trade policy, an efficiency objective voted through by the political track (other possible trade policies which would fit into this quadrant are analysed in Chapter 6). In contrast, option 3 represents shelter, an inefficient distribution-oriented policy favouring particular pressure groups again voted for explicitly by the political track.

Option 2 is where the United States perceives itself to be in the late twentieth century; exercising an efficiency-based trade policy through a technical track. For example, independent agencies conduct quasi-judicial investigations of the subsidies allegedly paid to foreigners by their governments. The agencies respond to petitions filed by domestic US firms who feel they suffer material injury from the subsidized imports.

In quadrant 4 the case is found whereby the pursuit of

distributional objectives is delegated to a technical track. In this context, we should recognize the intellectual possibility of an 'official' or intended trade policy located in quadrant 2, and an actual or realized trade policy in quadrant 4. Such a situation would imply that efficiency goals are subverted by the technical track which becomes subject to the influence of pressure groups. Hence distributional objectives are pursued in reality and unintended policy outcomes abound. The relevance of this particular quadrant 4 case will be demonstrated in Chapter 4 of this book, using the example of US trade policy. Indeed, a major point made (in effect) by the Canadian negotiating team in the recent bilateral trade negotiations between Canada and the United States was that the current administration of US trade remedy law placed it in quadrant 4 rather than in the intended quadrant 2.

Three problems exist with respect to pursuing efficiency-based objectives (the first and second option). First, even in the presence of clear efficiency-based objectives, the actual activities of sub-systems in the political and technical track may completely deviate from them. The resulting unintended trade policy outcomes will not necessarily be corrected because society has concerns other than merely trade policy criteria on its agenda. Such policies may be pursued because they generate high yields to specific pressure groups while their costs are spread over all taxpayers and consumers.[4]

Second, the political track in turn cannot be expected to eliminate such unintended policy outcomes in all circumstances. By definition it is subject to the pressure of political constituencies, whereby some constituencies may have more power to influence behaviour of the political track than others,[5] especially if its members are primarily guided by vote-maximizing considerations.[6] In this case the pursuit of distributional objectives may well dominate actual trade policy activities, in spite of the existence of efficiency-based objectives for trade policy.

The authority of the political track over the technical track can sometimes be extremely limited, namely when neither extensive cultural controls nor structural controls can be exerted on behaviour and only outputs can be controlled. Even then, the political track will often not be able to monitor all attributes of the technical track's outputs (which is a problem of comparative ignorance), so that the latter will be able to engage in discretionary behaviour.[7] Also, the political track, being guided to a large extent by vote-maximizing considerations, may want to use the technical track as a 'lightning conductor'. If the political track wishes to avoid being put under continuous pressure by specific constituenc-

that demand non-efficiency-based trade policy measures, then a meaningful alternative consists of completely delegating the implementation of trade policy to a public body that does not formally depend on a specific 'clientele'.

Third, the technical track, in cases where it is charged with implementing trade policy, may not, in practice, be able to pursue official trade policy ojectives. Its activities can only be monitored in a very limited way by the political track, so that bureau managers may, to a large extent, pursue their own objectives. Further, it may be put under pressure by the political track to perform activities which are conflicting with formal trade policy objectives. Finally, it may be influenced by its 'clientele'. Although the technical track is not directly accountable to political constituencies, it may well engage in collusive behaviour with specific pressure groups, as when it seeks to preserve its members' positions and budgets. Such behaviour can be expected if the technical track is used by the political track as a lightning conductor and pressure groups have easy access to it.

Although the political track may choose the first and second option, or a combination of both, in its policy formulation, the actual implementation of trade policy may deviate from the one that could be expected on the basis of national trade policy objectives. A distinction should thus be made between intended and unintended policy outputs, whereby the former are in accordance with the national trade policy objectives while the latter are not. If, for example, it is perceived that implementation of trade policy in the United States is actually located in cell 4, whereas officially it should be in cell 2, this presents a problem for both the United States and its major trading partners.[8] The empirical significance of this point will be demonstrated in the next sections.

Corporate influence on trade policy: the 1986 softwood lumber case

On the basis of the analysis performed in Chapter 2 and the previous section, we can now examine the strategies of firms aimed at influencing government trade policies. An important question to be answered is whether firms pursue the second or the fourth option (outlined in Figure 2.1). If the formulation of trade policy by government is assumed to be given at a specific point in time (Figure 3.1), then an analysis can be made of the influence of firms on the activities of the political and technical track, in terms of generating intended or unintended policy outputs. Particular attention must be paid to influence exerted on the technical track that leads to the creation of unintended policy outputs. Policy-improving measures should be taken if firms engaged in the fourth option generate high unintended policy outputs through influencing the activities of the technical track. In that case firms guided by non-efficiency-based strategies help in creating and sustaining trade policies with unintended policy outcomes.

We shall be concerned with the case where government is supposed to pursue efficiency-based trade policy objectives (formulation stage), but whereby some unintended policy outcomes can be observed in the implementation stage. This can occur when the behaviour of the technical track is partly guided by distributional considerations.[9] One particular example of the failure of the technical track and the politicization of US trade policy leading to unintended and inefficient policy outcomes is the 'Softwood Lumber from Canada' countervailing duty cases of 1982–3 and 1986.[10] In both cases the US lumber industry, mainly in the northwestern Pacific states, alleged that rival Canadian producers were receiving government subsidies (in the form of low provincial stumpage rates) in the production of timber, giving them an unfair cost advantage. Consequently the US industry requested that countervailing duties be imposed to offset the alleged degrees of subsidization.

Since under US trade law the importance of countervailing duties requires purely technical track investigations, there is no room for the President or Congress to be formally involved in the procedures. The US International Trade Commission (ITC) investigates and votes on material injury while the International Trade Administration (ITA) at the Department of Commerce undertakes a separate investigation to determine the nature and amount of the subsidy, and the extent of the countervailing duty to be levied on future imports of the product. In 1983 the ITC voted material injury, as it has done in 75 per cent of the preliminary decisions and 40 per cent of the final decisions of the Canadian cases brought before it.[11] However, the ITA determined that the Canadian provinces (which own the timber) set their stumpage rates in such a manner that they were 'generally available' to all users of timber products, regardless of the industry or enterprise of the recipient, and that any limitation on the industries actually using stumpage resulted only from the inherent characteristics of this natural resource. Thus, the ITA ruled that stumpage did not constitute an export subsidy and so was not subject to countervailing duties.

The 1983 case was lost on technical grounds, but the US lumber industry kept the issue alive by lobbying in Congress and various bills were presented which, if passed, would have allowed the United States to challenge the resource-pricing policies of sovereign foreign governments. In mid-1986 a second countervailing duty action against Canadian softwood lumber was introduced. Again the ITC voted material injury. This time, however, the ITA broadened the definition of countervailable subsidy and narrowed that of general availability, resulting in a reversal of its 1983 decision on general availability and an affirmative preliminary countervailing duty determination.

The origins of the change in the ITA's approach can be traced to a decision by the US Court of International Trade in October 1985 on a related appeal, the Cabot case. In that case, the Cabot Corporation, a US producer of carbon black, requested a review of a decision by the ITA, dealing with the Mexican government's provision of carbon black feedstock and natural gas to two Mexican producers of carbon black. The ITA had ruled in 1983 that the government set prices did not constitute a countervailable subsidy. The court decided, however, that the nominal general availability of benefits is not as important as the *de facto* benefits accruing to specific firms or industries. This decision was the basis of the misinformed and politicized ITA 1986 ruling on softwood lumber.

Realizing the threat that this precedent would pose for all resource-based exports to the United States, the Canadian federal government reached a political compromise with the US government which avoided the second and final stage of the ITA ruling. In accordance with the provinces and industries involved, the Canadian government agreed to impose an export tax equivalent to the 15 per cent countervail duty ruled by the ITA in its October report. This accommodation raised a political storm in Canada and it threatened, for a time, to disrupt the bilateral negotiations for a comprehensive free trade agreement.

Within the context of the analytical framework developed here, the softwood lumber case yields the following insights into the process of trade policy formulation and implementation. First, from Figure 2.1, the US lumber industry is adopting the fourth option, using the non-market environment to pursue a non-efficiency-based strategy. Second, in terms of Figure 3.1, policy formulation of the US administration, and even of Congress, involves mainly free trade (efficiency-based) objectives. Many documents state that the United States is a free trade nation and that it supports the objectives of GATT in liberalizing trade. The United States has also adopted a technical track process to implement its trade policy, so it believes itself to be in quadrant 2. However, third, it is apparent that the actual implementation of US trade policy is in quadrant 4 of Figure 3.1, generating high unintended policy outputs by the technical track.

The ITC and Commerce Department have both deviated from the technical track in the administration of trade law actions against Canada in recent years. In particular, proper economic analysis is not used by the ITC in voting material injury. This was demonstrated in the fresh Atlantic groundfish case of 1986 when injury was voted despite statistically insignificant questionnaire data and invalid analysis.[12] This tendency of US trade policy to be characterized by unintended policy outcomes is due to an excessive responsiveness to pressure groups. The softwood lumber case is a classic example of the abuse of the technical track because of its responsiveness to clientele needs. Yet it is not in the long-run interests of firms to seek the protection of the fourth option of Figure 2.1. Hence, it is now necessary to reform the administration of US trade policy so that the present ineffective decision structure is eliminated and implementation of US policy returns to conform with quadrant 2 of Figure 3.1.

The failure of the US technical track is a major problem for the trading partners of the United States, especially Canada. Throughout the free trade negotiations, the Canadian Trade Ambassador, Simon Reisman, in effect argued that the United States was in quadrant 4 of Figure 3.1. However, the US team believed they were in quadrant 2 of Figure 3.1. This led to the difficulty in reaching agreement, in October 1987, about the need for a binational panel to review countervail and anti-dumping actions.

The Canada–US Free Trade Agreement, however, contains a mechanism to alleviate this problem. A binational panel will provide exporters with a means to challenge trade policy implementation decisions of the importing country. The technical track will be less subject to pressure from clientele groups since its decisions (including all the economic evidence) can be reviewed by the panel. In this way the technical track will become more responsive to the government's official objectives and less subject to lobbying. Furthermore, option 4 in Figure 2.1 will no longer be as viable a strategy *vis-à-vis* Canadian exporters. Attempts by domestic firms to pursue non-efficiency-based strategies through government can be challenged by foreign rival firms upon which these trade penalties are being inflicted. If the domestic firms seeking shelter are unsuccessful, they will be forced to rationalize or exit the industry.

This binational panel is, however, only an interim solution. It should ensure that trade policy implementation is carried out scientifically in accordance with government objectives, i.e., that trade policy implementation does not create unintended policy outcomes. A proper subsidies code is still to be negotiated over a five- to seven-year period. This code should address the economics of trade remedy law and allow the binational panel to assess the net subsidy between plaintiff and defendant, not just the foreigners' subsidies, as is the current practice.

Problems in the administration of US trade law

The 'Softwood Lumber from Canada' case, discussed in the previous section, is a prime example of the sensitivity to clients of one body (the ITA) involved in the implementation of US trade policy. The 'Fresh Atlantic Groundfish from Canada' case, focusing on the International Trade Commission (ITC), provides further insight into the strategies of US firms to influence trade policy to their short-term advantage.

These cases are representative examples of the current use of US trade laws, which is a form of administered protection.[13] The present system of administered protection can be regarded as an example of administered market failure. Specific interest groups now stimulate the implementation of protectionist policy measures which profit only themselves in the short run. Such policies exist in contradiction to US free trade objectives.

It has also been demonstrated by others that US industries file petitions for protection when they face high import competition as a result of unfavourable comparative costs, i.e. when their FSAs have been eroded in an international context. In addition, a high 'complaints index' leads to significantly lower rates of import growth, which demonstrates the 'effectiveness' of these actions in terms of creating shelter.[14]

Trade policy implementation was first delegated to a technical track by Congress in 1934. This was done to shift the responsibility for trade policy measures to a forum in which no interest group bias would exist in favour of protectionism. In this sense, Congress insulated itself against its own tendency to subvert national free trade goals, which most members of Congress have supported over the last half century.[15]

After a careful analysis of the decision-making activities by the technical track in the Atlantic groundfish case, it was found that the rulings of 'material' injury were based on political and not on economic factors.[16] This is contradictory to US trade policy formulation which clearly emphasizes free trade goals and the principles of comparative advantage, statements which can be found in many other official US government policy documents. For example, the United States adopted the 'rules' of the GATT Tokyo Round on subsidies and countervailing duties (Subsidies Code) and the 1967 GATT code on anti-dumping duties (which was revised to include similar rules as the Subsidies Code). These require an objective economic analysis for the test of 'material injury' to the domestic industry in countervail and anti-dumping cases.

The GATT Subsidies Code states that a causal link must be established between the subsidized imports and the alleged material injury. Yet the ITC does not even test this link in most cases and it did not establish it at all when ruling on the Atlantic groundfish case. Moreover, the ITC reached its decision of material injury based on inconclusive evidence and a superficial analysis of the economic factors it is supposed to consider.[17] The ITC determination implies that inefficient US fishing companies with weak FSAs merely sought shelter from competition. The resulting duty imposed against Canadian imports suggests that these firms were able to influence decision making by the technical track.

US Trade law implementation: an inefficient outcome

The lessons of this case, and the softwood lumber case within the context of the theoretical framework developed in Chapter 2, are as follows. First, from Figure 2.1, the US fishing and lumber industries are pursuing non-efficiency-based strategies towards trade policy. Their prime purpose is to raise costs for foreign competitors. Such a strategy constitutes an important danger for firms with weak FSAs as explained by Figure 2.2. However, even companies with strong FSAs may well see their competitive strengths being eroded, as a result of relying on government shelter. By influencing government to impose protectionist trade policy measures they generate an uncompensated and unwilling transfer of wealth from foreign producers and domestic customers to themselves. Second, in terms of Figure 3.1, US trade policy formulation is in quadrant 2, i.e., strongly oriented towards free trade, but its implementation structure makes it sensitive to clientele needs. The strong pressure exerted by certain industries and firms to obtain shelter from foreign competition then leads to unintended trade policy outputs, which are in contradiction with US trade policy objectives.

One puzzle exists: why do firms engaging in efficiency strategies or consumers affected by protectionism not oppose protection? The main reason for this situation is the fact that benefits of protection accrue to a small number of firms, while producing only diffuse costs on most export industries or the general taxpayer and consumers.[18] In addition, export-oriented companies benefiting from strong FSAs may have more to gain from lobbying activities to receive government export support and other benefits building upon their FSAs than from fighting against import protection advocated by other firms.

Today, due to the strength of corporate pressure groups, the United States is sensitive to clientele needs. The impression may exist that, in general, the impact of specific pressure groups on policy implementation is low, as all cases undergo a formal, bureaucratic, two-track procedure. While it has long been recognized that the ITC is influenced by Congress, the ITA brought some balance to the technical track in the past.[19] The softwood lumber decision of 1986 was a bad precedent for US trade policy since it demonstrated the ease with which pressure groups could change trade policy implementation.

Although the Canadian government avoided a final determination from the ITA in the softwood lumber case by self-imposing a 15 per cent export tax on softwood lumber, the validity of the court decision in the Cabot case was not affected. The main problem with the administration of US trade law is that cases can be brought back to the technical track over and over again. Thus, even when a negative countervailable subsidy determination is decided, ultimately an affirmative determination can be granted. This affirmative ruling can then be used as a precedent for other cases in other industries.

It might still be argued that the technical track process regarding countervail and anti-dumping actions is not entirely biased against foreign producers, since a large number of cases do not result in a final positive determination of subsidy or dumping (see appendix to Chapter 4). Yet the occurrence of countervail and anti-dumping actions constitutes in itself an important protectionist tool: the riskiness of expected revenues of foreign exporters increases and substantial costs have to be borne when responding to complaints. Moreover, large administered protection actions (including safeguard actions) are sometimes a trigger for voluntary export restraints (for example in the automobile and steel case).

Finally, it is argued by some that countervail and anti-dumping actions are justified since they would create a level playing field. In reality, economic efficiency and consumer welfare, from a national point of view, are improved by the lower pricing of foreign firms.

Today, international competition from foreign exporters in global industries is mostly a guarantee for low prices, not high protected prices, in the domestic market. In this context it has been demonstrated that, for example, most US countervail cases occurred in industries with many suppliers.[20]

The United States now has a trade policy implementation structure whereby any industry or even a single firm can trigger protectionist measures at negligible monetary costs. In this way, the United States is now engaged on a path of increasing protectionist trade policy measures, to shelter domestic producers from global competition. Such a government trade policy strategy is beneficial neither to the nation as a whole nor to the firms pursuing non-efficiency-based strategies.

Conclusion

The application of the framework developed in Chapter 2 allowed us to gain conceptual insights into the interactive nature of corporate strategies and government trade policies in the United States. It was documented that the pressure exerted on government by firms engaging in a non-efficiency-based strategy may constitute an important problem in a country like the United States with free trade goals. If the implementation structure is very sensitive to clientele demands, this implies that national trade policy goals are subverted and unintended long-run policy outcomes are generated.

We demonstrated, through the use of two Canadian case studies, that the present system of administered protection in the United States corresponds precisely to such a situation. In addition, it appears that trade law implementation by the political track itself is also subject to non-efficiency-based strategies, especially from weak firms in declining industries. Firms and industries engaging in non-efficiency-based strategies are able to exert influence on government to realize shelter through trade barriers against foreign competition. In a world of increased global competition such actions will only weaken the competitive strengths of the sectors involved. Granting shelter to these companies is not a solution that will improve their competitive advantages in the long run. Instead, it may well affect adversely their long-term prospects of survival, profit and growth. In the next chapter, we will investigate how Canadian firms have responded to increasing administered protection in the United States.

Chapter four

Corporate strategy for trade barriers

The Canadian corporate response to US trade policies

This chapter investigates the links between the international trade and investment strategies of Canadian firms competing in a regulated global environment and faced with rising US protectionism. A modified framework is developed to analyse the strategic alternatives available to firms when dealing with government policies. This builds upon the concepts of corporate strategy and entry barriers discussed below. The framework is used to discover how administered protection, especially in the United States, is the result of interactive behaviour beween business and government.

This type of protection can severely change the environment for corporations when used as a strategic weapon by domestic firms against foreign rivals. However, the earlier framework developed in Chapter 2 only recognized the existence of corporate behaviour aimed at creating or maintaining government-induced entry barriers for foreign competitors. This applies to firms in quadrants 2 and 4 of Figure 2.1. In contrast, the new framework developed here acknowledges two other possibilities. The first is that certain firms may still perceive trade policy as an environmental parameter beyond their control. The second possibility is that some firms may attempt to eliminate existing trade barriers of benefit to foreign rivals. In other words their objective is not to create but to abolish entry barriers. We also recognize the possibility that corporate strategies may achieve different levels of success in actually influencing trade policy outcomes.

In the past decade, as the use of tariff barriers has declined, they have been replaced by forms of non-tariff protectionism. Administered protection through anti-dumping actions and the imposition of countervailing duties has increased, particularly in the United States. This escalation in administered forms of protection is explained in more detail in the Appendix to this chapter.

Hence, we now assess in detail the response of Canadian firms faced with the recent rise of US-administered protection. We demonstrate how they have been able to influence government policy in order to diminish the impact of US protectionism. We also address the question of why certain Canadian firms oppose trade liberalization between the United States and Canada, in spite of US-administered protection. We show how they have been able to influence the Canadian government to retain 'artificial' competitive advantages.

Canadian firms may attempt to retain protectionist measures as a tool of competitive strategy to deter entry into their home market by foreign rivals. It is also shown that firms may stimulate government to eliminate trade barriers so that competition can take place on the basis of micro-economic efficiency and natural comparative advantage. This recognizes that policy measures such as changes in trade barriers are not merely environmental factors, beyond the control of business, but variables which firms can influence. Trade policy is an instrument of competitive strategy for Canadian firms as well as for their rivals in other nations.

Corporate strategy and trade policy

Several authors have discussed the increasing importance of global competition and triad power,[1] i.e. intense competition between the firms of three economic powers: the United States, Japan and the European Community. For business located in small open economies, which do not form a part of the triad, it then becomes of paramount importance to secure access to the market of at least one of the triad powers. This is essential for long-term survival, profitability and growth.

If firms of small open economies are confronted with protectionism imposed by one (or more) of the triad powers, internalization theory suggests that companies with strong FSAs can overcome these government regulations by engaging in foreign direct investment.[2] However, protectionism still affects the global strategies of firms as well as influencing their choice of mode for servicing the triad power markets. This is so for two reasons. First, protection can be influenced by firms. Second, trade and foreign direct investment may be complements, so free trade constitutes an important determinant of global competitiveness.

The hypothesis that trade policy may be influenced by firms is supported by a wide body of theoretical and empirical literature, some of it already synthesized in earlier sections of this book. It has been demonstrated that specific interest groups can affect government policies: trade protection then serves private interests at the expense of society at large.[3] Also relevant to an understanding of global competition is the so-called comparative costs model.[4] This model suggests that comparatively efficient industries which are export-oriented will advocate the elimination of trade barriers, while comparatively inefficient industries will attempt to increase or maintain trade barriers.

The new public choice theory takes into account the possibility that some firms may want to eliminate trade barriers, as this would allow them to compete on the basis of their micro-economic efficiency. But the analysis neglects the fact that influencing trade policy primarily results from strategic decisions made by firms, not industries. If it is assumed that trade policy preferences mainly exist at the firm level and that, in certain cases, individual companies may indeed influence the outcomes of trade policy, Figure 4.1 can be constructed.

Four different cases can be distinguished, as represented in Figure 4.1. The horizontal axis identifies the corporation's strategic preferences with respect to the existence of trade barriers and the vertical axis determines whether trade policy outcomes are perceived as controllable by the firm. If trade policy outcomes are perceived as controllable this implies that they may be influenced through strategic management decisions.

In the context of global competition, Figure 4.1 is of major importance to the managers of firms operating in international markets. For each country in which they compete they can position their firm in one of the four quadrants of Figure 4.1. Such global trade policy analysis can also be performed at the business unit level. However, this could lead to internal tensions in the organization if different business units were to advocate opposite positions about their preferences on changes in trade barriers.

In terms of actual behaviour at the country level, it is clear that corporate positions in quadrants 2 and 4 will lead to strategic actions aimed at influencing trade barriers. Strategic behaviour meant to decrease trade barriers (quadrant 2) implies that a firm attempts to eliminate 'artificial' competitive advantages of benefit to foreign rivals. In contrast, attempts to increase (or maintain) protection may be motivated in three ways:

1 either a firm does not want to compete on the basis of market forces and has a preference for erecting artificial entry barriers against foreign competitors (non-efficiency strategy – quadrant 4 in Figure 2.1); or

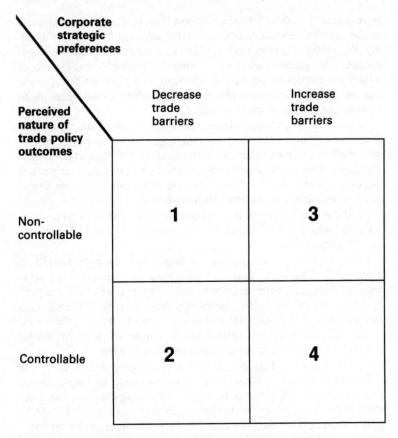

Figure 4.1 Strategy formulation and protection

2   a firm wants to achieve a level playing field, whereby it wishes
    to receive the same artificial advantages accruing to foreign
    rivals (efficiency strategy – quadrant 2 in Figure 2.1); or
3   a firm has a preference for trade barriers building upon its
    FSAs, for example, in the infant industry case (secondary non-
    efficiency strategy – quadrant 4 in Figure 2.1 complementing
    a long-run efficiency strategy in quadrants 1 or 2).

There is, however, a crucial distinction to be made between the
intended impact of corporate strategic management on trade
policy outcomes and its realized impact, as demonstrated in Figure
4.2. Whereas Figure 4.1 can be considered as a useful tool when

developing strategies towards trade policy outcomes (*ex ante*), Figure 4.2 relates intended impacts to realized impacts. The vertical axis of Figure 4.2 should be considered as a continuum where firms can determine the level of consistency between the trade policy outcomes hoped for and the actual impact of their actions. Hence this axis provides a measure of the effectiveness of corporate strategic management towards government trade policy.

From a global perspective, this analysis can again be made for each country in which an active strategy towards trade policy was pursued. Differences in consistency between intended and realized impacts among countries may then lead to a global learning effect

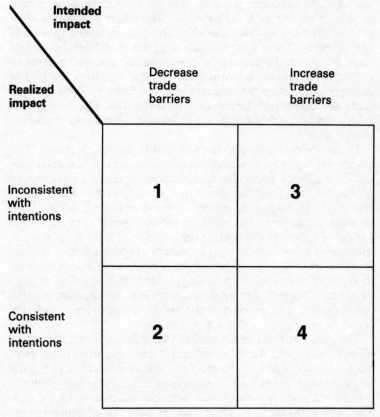

Figure 4.2 Corporate impact on trade policy outcomes

about which actions are most effective, although this depends on the particular institutional structure within which trade policy in a particular country is conducted. Such learning effects will exist especially for firms attempting to reduce trade barriers in order to facilitate exports. It will be less important for firms that pursue the erection of trade barriers, as the search for government protection is often an indicator of failure to be internationally competitive. As a result, the firm's market becomes restricted to the home country.

The key question is whether exports and foreign direct investment are substitutes or complements. Only in the latter case (and in cases where exports and investments are imperfect substitutes) does it make economic sense for efficient firms to seek the elimination of trade barriers, as this would affect their world-wide competitive position *vis-à-vis* global rivals. The argument that trade and investment are complements suggests that liberalization of trade promotes the growth of economic activity, which leads to greater investment opportunities at the country level. For example, the EC experienced rapid increases in both internal trade and direct investment after its formation. There were also greater inflows of third party investment, especially from the United States.[5]

Trade liberalization also implies that firms must increase their efforts towards global rationalization. This means that each subsidiary is given a particular specialization in the vertical chain of production. On the other hand, the absence of free trade forces companies to engage in excessive horizontal integration. Then subsidiaries in protected markets produce small runs to a wide variety of products, preventing the creation of scale economies or specialized know-how in the production of specific items. Rationalization implies that the subsidiary is being used as one element in a global cost leadership strategy with global sourcing, instead of having a protected market strategy itself. An alternative is the granting of world product mandates to subsidiaries, which are then meant to pursue global focus strategies.

The above analysis demonstrates that efficient firms, competing globally, may well derive significant advantages from the elimination of trade barriers. Finally, in certain industries, especially resource-based ones (where processing is limited), foreign direct investment may not constitute a viable alternative to exports. Then the elimination of trade barriers becomes of prime importance to the companies involved.

Corporate strategy and administered protection in this model

As shown in earlier chapters, under US trade law, domestic producers can now launch actions to initiate countervailing duty and anti-dumping investigations against rival foreign producers. We have shown earlier, using the framework developed in Chapter 2, that such cases of administered protection are in quadrant 4, rather than quadrant 2, of Figure 2.1. US companies thereby engage in protected market strategies and create substantial entry barriers for corporations exporting to the United States.[6] The realized impact of this corporate strategy is becoming increasingly consistent with its intended impact. The ITC and ITA are tools for strategic planners of inefficient US firms to obtain shelter from global competition. By the very nature of the ITC and ITA, the realized impact of such strategies is biased towards being consistent with the intentions of these protection-seeking firms.

The lessons to be learned from the present use of US administered protection within the context of the theoretical framework developed in this chapter, are as follows. First, in Figure 4.1, US industries such as fishing, lumber and steel are pursuing a quadrant 4 strategy (which, in this case, is equivalent to quadrant 4 of Figure 2.1). Their primary purpose is to raise entry barriers for foreign competitors. They can do this by use of the non-exogenous technical route of US-administered protection, a system which they use to obtain shelter. Second, in terms of Figure 4.2, these US firms are also in quadrant 4, which implies that US trade policy implementation is sensitive to clientele needs. The question then arises as to what actions can be taken by efficient foreign producers from small open economies such as Canada to eliminate the negative impact of such protectionism?

Corporate responses in Canada to US-administered protection

Data were gathered on the views of senior management of large Canadian firms towards possible trade liberalization between the US and Canada.[7] A first survey included the largest Canadian multinational enterprises and the largest US subsidiaries in Canada. The questionnaire was sent to the chief executive officer of each of these firms in April 1987.[8] The strategic planners in each of these companies were asked questions about the impact of trade liberalization on their competitive strategies.

The single most important finding of this questionnaire is that trade liberalization will be welcomed by these multinationals to the extent that it will create access to the US market. Hence, it is clear that free trade is favoured by the Canadian multinationals. Seventy-five per cent of them indicated that a Canada–US free trade agreement would be beneficial to them. The basis of this support for free trade is rooted in the prevailing view that the status quo is one of increasing protectionism in the United States. Sixty-three per cent of these firms indicate that the status quo in Canada–US trade relations does not benefit them. The questionnaire also yielded indications about the process of adjustment. Seventy-five per cent of the respondents indicated that they would not close plants in Canada because of a free trade agreement. In fact, in the forecasting section, 50 per cent of the Canadian firms expect their investments to increase in Canada between 10 and 20 per cent after five years of the agreement, indicating that trade and investment are complements.

After the actual negotiations of the Free Trade Agreement were completed, another survey was administered to the list of firms. This survey, administered in the spring of 1988, yielded results similar to those from the first survey. These firms, responding in light of the final text of the agreement, again overwhelmingly supported bilateral free trade. These strong results indicate that the Canadian MNEs have efficient internal strategic management mechanisms to help pilot their firms to a new regime of bilateral free trade and would be located on the left-hand side of Figure 4.1. These survey results also confirm earlier analysis that adjustment to Canada–US free trade is already underway in Canadian-owned multinationals. An in-depth analysis of this issue can be found in Chapter 5.

While these questionnaires survey large corporations, surveys of small business by the Canadian Federation of Independent Business (CFIB) have reported similar results (CFIB 1988). The CFIB found that its members believed that the Agreement would have a positive or neutral effect on their business. In fact, the ratio of these responses to negative beliefs was overwhelming at nine to one.

It appears that most of the larger firms have adopted a strategy in quadrant 2 of Figure 4.1 partly because they were confronted with the major issue of US-administered protection. It was precisely the rise of protectionist tendencies in the United States which led many broad-based industry groups, including the Canadian Manufacturers' Association, to drop their indifference or outright opposition to free trade and become strong advocates of a bilateral trade agreement. This change in attitude reflected the negative effects of US trade law actions upon the interests of the Canadian private sector, especially exporters. These included

Canadian forestry, agriculture, steel and mineral resource producers.

When the Canadian government decided to negotiate a comprehensive bilateral trade agreement in September 1985, the private sector did indeed exercise a major influence on the outcome of the trade talks. This overall position of Canadian businesses in favour of the Free Trade Agreement was made possible by the result of an institutional structure set up to advise the Federal Government on this issue. This structure consisted of the International Trade Advisory Committee (ITAC), set up in January 1986 to advise the Minister of International Trade and the government on the broad policy aspects of bilateral and multilateral (GATT) trade negotiations. In addition, fifteen Sectoral Advisory Groups on International Trade (SAGITs) were established in August 1986 to serve as repositories of information about their own sectors. The process of participation in trade policy formulation provided a two-way flow of information and most of the SAGITs supported the government's trade policy initiative.

Having established that the strategic preference of most Canadian corporations was in favour of trade liberalization and that an institutional framework was set up which allowed them to perceive trade policy as non-exogenous, it only remains to be seen if the intended impact of these firms was consistent with the realized impact. The Free Trade Agreement obviously does not completely solve the problem of rising protectionism in the United States, although a new bilateral dispute settlement mechanism (introduced on 1 January 1989) may contribute to offset abusive trade law procedures in either country.[9]

As stated earlier, the new binational panel puts in place a mechanism for Canada to influence, and potentially change, the investigative practices of the US ITC and the US Commerce Department (ITA) in their gathering of data and analysis. Article 1904(2) of the Free Trade Agreement provides for a panel review based upon the 'administrative record' which is defined in Article 1911 as including 'all documentary or other information presented to or obtained by the competent investigating authority'.[10] Members of the panel will be able to review the administrative practice used to deal with material constituting the administrative record and bring their expertise to bear on the question of whether this information was dealt with properly. In this way economic evidence (already put on the administrative record by defence lawyers) can be reviewed by the binational panel. This should lead to increased use of rational economics-based tests and decreased clientele power during technical track investigations.

Not all Canadian firms, however, have the same strategic preference. Litvak found that broad-based associations, such as the
Business Council on National Issues and the Canadian Organization of Small Business, have been the leading proponents of a
comprehensive bilateral trade agreement between Canada and the
United States (Litvak 1986). They see secure Canadian access to
the US market as vital to maintaining Canada's standard of living.
Litvak also found that industry-specific associations are less unified
in their attitudes towards a bilateral trade agreement. His work
suggests that the broader groups use arguments based on general
economic principles, while individual sector positions depend on
special factors. Several associations revealed multiple positions on
the free trade issue, due to their diversity in size and predis-
position towards economic nationalism, or to the multiple participation by their members in industry sub-sectors or markets. Thus,
a minority of Canadian firms adopted a quadrant 4 corporate
strategy in Figure 4.1. With the signing of the Free Trade Agreement it appears that the influence exerted by firms in quadrant 2 of
Figure 4.1 was substantially stronger than the impact of Canadian
companies in favour of maintaining trade barriers, putting the
former in quadrant 2 of Figure 4.2.

However, not all firms and industries located in the fourth
quadrant of Figure 4.1 were unsuccessful in terms of realized
impacts (quadrant 3 of Figure 4.2). Industries such as the brewing
industry, and segments of the agricultural industry protected by
marketing boards, were exempted from the Free Trade Agreement, indicating that they were able to position themselves in
quadrant 4 of Figure 4.2. This shows that they were sufficiently
powerful to be bought off in order not to oppose the free trade
deal. Other industries, such as the grape-growing and wine-
producing industry in Ontario, which also attempted to oppose
bilateral trade liberalization, were not able to secure permanent
shelter. Faced with increased US competition, their strategic
alternatives are now to exit or to improve their economic
efficiency. This conclusion is important as it indicates that
the pursuit of efficiency and the development of lobbying activities to reduce competition through trade barriers are in fact
strategic alternatives for managers faced with international
competition.

Important strategic activities located in quadrant 2 of Figure
2.1 should still be developed by Canadian and other firms wishing
to develop stable access to the US market. Kymlicka has studied
how Canadian steel firms attempted to prevent the imposition of
protectionist measures against their exports to the United States

(Kymlicka 1987). He demonstrated the need for these firms to engage in individual and industry-wide lobbying to defend and promote their interests both in Canada and the United States. He argued, in accordance with our analysis of trade policy protectionism in the United States, that a sheltering strategy is now widely used by American firms positioned in quadrant 4 of both Figures 4.1 and 4.2. Hence, it appears to be crucial for foreign firms, exporting to the United States and positioned in quadrant 2 of Figure 4.1, to develop active strategies aimed at securing a place in quadrant 2, instead of quadrant 1, in Figure 4.2.

The rise of other types of protection in the United States

Chapter 3, as well as previous sections of this chapter, mainly dealt with the issue of administered protection through the abusive use of unfair trade law by US firms seeking shelter. Some data on anti-dumping and countervail actions initiated both by the United States and by other nations is described in the Appendix to this chapter. In practice, government shelter can also be acquired through many other types of protectionist actions in the realm of trade policy. Five different legal paths can be used to obtain shelter.

1 Exceptionally high tariffs, largely legacies from the period before World War Two (for example tariffs first introduced through the Fordney–McCumber Tariff Act of 1922 and the Smoot–Hawley Tariff Act of 1930). Examples of industries that were able to retain tariffs on imports of at least 15 per cent in the 1980s include, for example, benzenoid chemicals, rubber footware, textiles and apparel. The level of tariffs in these industries contrasts sharply with the average ratio of duties collected to dutiable imports which dropped from 53.5 per cent in 1933 to approximately 5.2 per cent in 1982.
2 Escape clause relief granted by the President of the United States, based on the advice of the ITC (for speciality steel, colour televisions and motorcycles, for example).
3 Presidential use of inherent institutional powers (for example voluntary restraint agreements on steel exports from countries such as the EC, Japan, Korea and Brazil).
4 Statutory frameworks for discretionary protection, especially the use of countervailing and anti-dumping actions which are the main focus of this book.
5 Statutory quotas limiting imports or even banning foreign firms

from the US market (such as the Jones Act in the marine sector).

The costs of corporate shelter are a large burden on the US economy. In 1984, these five types of special protection represented a direct cost of US$53 billion to US consumers (not taking into account X-efficiency implications).[11] In 1984, the share of total imports affected by the sheltering policies described above was 21 per cent (or US$67.6 billion) up from 8 per cent in 1975 and 12 per cent in 1980. It was calculated that the decrease of imports induced by the five forms of shelter described above amounted to US$44.4 billion in 1984.[12] Other calculations of the World Bank indicate that approximately 15 per cent of US imports from industrial countries were affected by non-tariff barriers and voluntary restraint arrangements in 1986, up from 9 per cent in 1981. The figures for imports from developing countries are 17 per cent for 1986 and 14 per cent for 1981. These percentages should be considered as minima since they only include the portion of imports from the countries affected by the export restraints and not the entire product sector affected by this shelter.[13]

These figures demonstrate the costs that US firms imposed on US consumers through the development of non-efficiency strategies. Similar costs occur in other nations where shelter is practised. Of course, not all of these measures have completely failed in the long run. The US escape clause has performed reasonably well because the relief granted has always been temporary (four years on average), thus stimulating firms to maintain a long-run efficiency-based strategy. As a result, the escape clause has mostly led to strong adjustment, usually associated with contracting to a competitive core.[14] In other words, firms benefiting from the escape clause have sometimes been forced to develop an efficiency-based strategy instead of a shelter-based one.[15]

Conclusion

The analytical framework developed here is used to demonstrate how Canadian firms can influence national trade policy through their corporate strategy. With the aid of two matrices it is again shown that an increasing number of US firms are seeking and obtaining administered protection, which places them in quadrant 4 of these figures. Recognizing the threat this poses to their viability in a world of triad power, most Canadian firms have taken steps to design strategies to place themselves in quadrant 2 of Figure 4.1. Through the Canada–US Free Trade Agreement, these firms will largely achieve their goal of reducing trade barriers into the US market. They must then continue with this strategy in order to obtain a proper Canada–United States Subsidies Code. Other Canadian firms, fearing competition from US rivals under trade liberalization, have placed themselves in quadrant 4 of Figure 4.1. Many of these were successful in maintaining trade barriers for their respective industries. However, to ensure long-run survival, without shelter, in a world of increasing global competition, these firms must develop their FSAs to become competitive in the international marketplace.

Appendix to Chapter 4
Data on anti-dumping and countervail actions
prepared by Thomas M. Boddez

This appendix reports and examines data on the degree to which anti-dumping and countervailing duty actions have been used since the 1979 Tokyo Round of the General Agreement on Tariffs and Trade established a subsidies code and new procedures for the administration of these trade remedy laws by member countries.

Anti-dumping

The use of anti-dumping actions is listed in Table 4A.1. This table shows all anti-dumping investigations initiated between January 1980 and 30 June 1988. All 1,255 actions during this period were initiated by either the EC, or one of the ten other countries listed. Over 97 per cent of all actions were initiated by four groups: the United States, Australia, Canada, and the EC. Leading the way is the United States, with 384 actions initiated during the period being studied. This is 30.6 per cent, almost one-third, of all actions undertaken. Australia is next with 25.34 per cent, followed by Canada at 22.71 per cent and the EC at 18.96 per cent.

From the figures in Table 4A.1, it can be concluded that the United States and the EC, two of the three triad powers, are characterized by a form of protectionism which must be taken into consideration by any corporate strategy which contemplates penetration of these markets. Interestingly, the third member of the triad, Japan, does not use anti-dumping at all. A possible explanation for this is the existence of cultural and related environmental factors making such retaliatory measures unnecessary.

Table 4A.1 Anti-dumping actions initiated by country, 1 January 1980 to 30 June 1988

Country	1980	1980–1	1981–2	1982–3	1983–4	1984–5	1985–6	1986–7	1987–8	TOTAL	Percentage of actions
US	37	15	50	40	46	61	63	41	31	384	30.60%
Australia	0	0	0	71	70	63	54	40	20	318	25.34%
Canada	26	29	64	34	26	35	27	24	20	285	22.71%
EC	17	22	36	26	33	34	23	17	30	238	18.96%
Finland	0	2	0	0	1	0	0	5	5	13	1.04%
Korea	0	0	0	0	0	0	3	1	0	4	0.32%
Sweden	0	0	2	0	0	0	2	0	0	4	0.32%
New Zealand	0	0	0	0	0	0	0	0	4	4	0.32%
Austria	1	1	0	0	0	0	0	0	0	2	0.16%
Mexico	0	0	0	0	0	0	0	0	2	2	0.16%
Brazil	0	0	0	0	0	0	0	0	1	1	0.08%
Yearly total	81	69	152	171	176	193	172	128	113	1,255	100.00%

Source: GATT 1980–8

Notes: Reports are made to GATT on a semi-annual basis. The reporting period for 1980 above only covers from 1 January 1980 to 30 June 1980. All other columns are from 1 July of the preceding year to 30 June of the following year. 'Percentage of actions' column shows the proportion of actions which were undertaken by each GATT signatory over the entire period from 1 January 1980–30 June 1988.

Countervailing duties

The use of countervailing duties as a protectionist measure is detailed in Table 4A.2. Again, the time period extends from January 1980 to 30 June 1988. Only six countries plus the EC used countervail measures during this period; however, the statistical breakdown is much more concentrated than it was in the case of anti-dumping. Two countries, the United States and Chile, are responsible for 89.31 per cent of all countervail cases initiated during this period. The United States initiated 304 of the 496 cases reported to GATT, or 61.29 per cent. Chile initiated 139 of the 496 cases, or 28.02 per cent. No other country, including the EC, was responsible for more than 4.64 per cent of the cases.

Table 4A.2 shows that the United States is the only triad power to use countervailing measures extensively to protect domestic industries. In the case of anti-dumping, use was spread among four main users including the EC, but the United States has been the overwhelming leader in the use of countervail. This becomes increasingly evident when we take a closer look at Chile, the only other significant countervail user. Although they have initiated 139 actions in the past, only one of these cases ever reached an affirmative final determination.[16] In contrast, US cases often result in the imposition of duties. This means that closer to 90 per cent of effective CVD cases are initiated by the United States, making countervailing duties almost exclusively a US phenomenon. Given this fact, the close analysis of US-administered protection undertaken in this study is clearly warranted.

The nature of US-administered protection

Table 4A.3 reveals in more detail the degree of administered protection exhibited by US companies towards rival firms in other countries or regions. As it is based on data from the US International Trade Commission (ITC) Annual Reports, the table captures a slightly longer time period (January 1980–September 1988) than the GATT data (January 1980–June 1988). Problems in comparability also stem from differences in ITC listings and GATT listings; however, this does not hamper the relevance of Table 4A.3, which identifies the targets of US-administered protection.

Table 4A.3 reports 431 anti-dumping cases initiated by the United States under section 731 of the Trade Agreements Act, of which 140 resulted in the imposition of duties. Thus 33 per cent of all anti-dumping investigations led to affirmative rulings. The

Table 4A.2 Countervail actions initiated by country, 1 January 1980 to 30 June 1988

Country	1980	1980–1	1981–2	1982–3	1983–4	1984–5	1985–6	1986–7	1987–8	Total	Percentage of actions
US	40	7	75	35	22	60	41	11	13	304	61.29%
Chile	0	0	66	33	19	10	11	0	0	139	28.02%
Australia	0	0	0	9	3	5	3	3	0	23	4.64%
Canada	3	3	0	2	3	2	1	4	0	18	3.63%
EC	1	0	1	3	1	0	0	0	0	7	1.41%
New Zealand	0	0	0	0	0	0	0	1	4	5	1.01%
Japan	0	0	0	1	0	0	0	0	0	1	0.20%
Yearly total	44	10	142	83	48	77	56	19	17	496	100.00%

Source: Gatt 1980–7 and 1988
Notes: Reports are made to GATT on a semi-annual basis. The reporting period identified for 1980 above consists of 1 January 1980–30 June 1980. All other columns are from 1 July of the preceding year to 30 June of the following year. 'Percentage of actions' column shows the proportion of actions which were undertaken by each GATT signatory over the entire period from 1 January 1980 to 30 June 1988.

Table 4A.3 Number of US countervail and anti-dumping cases against other nations, 1980–8

Region and country	Anti-dumping cases		Countervail cases	
	Initiated	Final positive	Initiated	Final positive
North America				
Canada	22	9	17	4
Mexico	7	2	4	1
Latin America	53	18	56	20
European Community	138	25	196	38
Other Western Europe	21	5	31	7
Eastern Europe	36	7	0	0
Asia				
Japan	55	26	6	0
South Korea	24	11	16	7
Taiwan	26	12	7	1
People's Republic of China	16	11	0	0
Other Asian	15	7	15	2
Pacific	5	1	5	0
Africa	8	2	1	0
Middle East	5	3	5	3
Total US actions	431	140	369	83

Source: US International Trade Commission, *Annual Report*, 1980–8. Period covered is from 1 October 1979 to 30 September 1988.

table also shows 369 countervail cases initiated. These include countervail investigations under Sections 701, 303, and 104 of the Trade Agreements Act. A total of 83 of these resulted in final affirmative rulings, for a 22.5 per cent success rate.

In terms of competitive strategy, the most interesting information in the table is the breakdown of countries suffering from such US actions. The European Community, with 138 anti-dumping and 196 countervail cases initiated against it, is the biggest target. Latin America, Japan, Canada, other Western European nations, South Korea, and Taiwan are the next most heavily penalized areas. Countervail cases have seldom been used by the United States against Japan, where anti-dumping cases are the main protectionist measure. In contrast, countervail is used more extensively than is anti-dumping against the other triad power, the EC.

The data in Table 4A.3 show that the United States has corporations which use both countervailing and anti-dumping measures in an extensive manner. This creates some special problems for corporate strategic planners.

Implications for strategic planning

Corporate strategic planners of global firms cannot afford to ignore the effects of administered protection on trading patterns today. From an export perspective, the threat of administered protection can increase the costs of developing a foreign market, as the risk of duties or restraints being imposed must be considered as well as the legal and administrative costs which could be incurred while fighting the imposition of the action.[17] This could, in some cases, lead to more foreign direct investment (FDI) in order to circumvent the threat of export restraints. From the domestic perspective, strategic planners, particularly for internationally uncompetitive firms, can use the system as a strategic weapon to protect their market from foreign competitors.

However, it is important to remember that administered protection often makes little economic sense. In the case of anti-dumping, one of the main reasons cited in defence of its use is to offset the effects of predatory pricing on the part of foreign firms. Proponents of this theory fear that foreign firms will become dominant in the domestic economy, and then raise prices substantially. However, by using anti-dumping legislation, the same result occurs. A domestic firm which successfully lobbies for protection now has a protected market and a more monopolistic position than would otherwise have been the case, and the domestic players are in a position to charge higher prices and survive in spite of inefficiency.[18]

Turning to countervail, imposition of duties in opposition to foreign subsidies decreases the welfare of consumers. Political pressure plays a large role in the process, due to the ability of firms to organize and successfully lobby for their own benefit despite the welfare loss for the diffuse and non-vocal public. Unfortunately, the test of whether or not material injury has actually occurred is not given the attention it deserves.

While the use of administered protection affects corporate strategic planning globally, it must be reiterated that the United States presents the greatest obstacle. With its decentralized political and administrative system, the United States is very susceptible to lobbying pressures, making it the leader in imposition of both anti-dumping and countervailing duties. Thus, corporate strategists must be most cautious when entering this market. The issue of administered protection is less important when dealing with the EC, and not important at all in regard to Japan.

Chapter five

Global corporate strategy and the Free Trade Agreement

Sources of competitive advantage

In order to interpret the impact of the Canada–US Free Trade Agreement on the strategies of MNEs, we need an analytical framework that can incorporate factors particular to the firm as well as to the country.[1] In the first chapter we already argued that a firm's potential competitiveness depends upon its firm-specific advantages (FSAs). These FSAs refer to the core skills and know-how of a company, i.e. its distinctive competencies.

The use of FSAs within the context of a corporation constitutes a first source of competitive advantage, whether cost or differentiation based. FSAs, of course, only create the *potential* for actual competitive advantage in the marketplace. Only through the effective formulation and implementation of competitive strategies can FSAs be translated into cost or differentiation advantages. FSAs are thus the key source for obtaining competitive advantages in the market-place. However, the potential competitive advantages which can be achieved also depend upon country-specific advantages (CSAs) facing the firm. The CSAs represent country characteristics that may give the firm an edge (strong CSA) or a disadvantage (weak CSA) *vis-à-vis* foreign rivals. Thus, tariff and non-tariff barriers to trade may constitute a CSA for protected firms in the domestic market. Environmental factors such as resource availability can also be a key CSA.

It is through the use of competitive strategies that firms turn these FSAs and CSAs into actual competitive advantages in the market-place. In the Canadian case, our focus must be on the multinational enterprises, which account for the majority of international trading activity.[2] Building on the available pool of CSAs and FSAs, the MNE makes decisions about the optimal global configuration and coordination of its value-added chain (operations, marketing, R&D and logistics). In fact, the skill in making

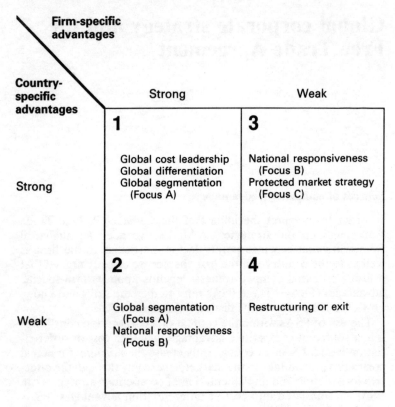

Figure 5.1 Competitive strategies in global industries

these decisions may in itself constitute a strong managerial FSA. In this context it has been found that most Canadian MNEs have strong resource-based CSAs and differentiation-enhancing FSAs.[3]

Competitive strategies in global industries

Recognizing that there are different strategic avenues to success, it is useful to distinguish between Canadian firms based on the relative strengths of their CSAs and FSAs, as in Figure 5.1. This allows for the classification of firms in global industries according to their competitive strategies. Global industries are defined here as industries characterized by strong international competition and intra-industry trade. In this matrix, 'strength' is a relative notion. A strong FSA means that the company has the potential to erect sustainable entry barriers against foreign rivals, so as to secure its product-market domain. A strong CSA reflects the potential to be competitive against international rivals, but its source lies outside the firm (for example cheap and abundant labour, efficiency of the capital market, high-quality human capital, abundant natural resources, or government shelter).

The competitive strategy matrix for global industries is amenable to the generic competitive strategy work by Porter. He demonstrates that firms in global industries can pursue strategies of global cost leadership, global differentiation and focus (Porter 1986). The focus strategy itself consists of three possible options. First, there is global segmentation (focus A) whereby the firm pursues cost leadership or differentiation in many geographic markets but only in a selected number of market segments. Second, a firm may follow a national responsiveness (focus B) strategy, whereby cost leadership or differentiation is targeted in a limited number of market segments, but only in one (or a few) geographic market(s). Finally, a protected market (focus C) strategy can be pursued. With this strategy, the firm's domain is primarily based in one country, but the segment scope may be very large. A competitive advantage is gained against global rivals as a result of government shelter. Here, the firm's main competitive advantage is not cost- or differentiation-based, but results from the government imposing artificial costs on foreign rivals. Hence, this strategy could be referred to as the 'fourth generic'. Cell 1 firms generally can follow any of the three generic strategies described above. If they choose a focus strategy, however, it will probably be a global segmentation (focus A) strategy. With their international competitive advantages they will be able to penetrate many foreign markets with all product lines that share strong FSAs and CSAs.

Firms in cell 2 will mostly confine themselves to some form of focus if they are faced with global competitors benefiting from strong CSAs. The relative disadvantage of such operations can only be compensated by reducing their geographic or segment scope, i.e. by developing some form of specialization in order to beat their rivals that benefit from strong FSAs and CSAs simultaneously. An alternative is of course to shift operations completely towards countries characterized by strong CSAs, but this is not always possible in cases of high exit barriers, foreign governments' discriminatory policies in favour of domestic firms and in cases where exports and foreign direct investment are imperfect substitutes. We should recognize, however, that conceptually it is possible for strong FSAs to compensate largely for the existence of weak CSAs,[4] thus allowing the pursuit of global cost leadership or differentiation.

Cell 3 firms are generally confined to a more limited geographic market domain except when producing a largely generic product, where FSAs have become unimportant (for example in cases where the products are in a late stage in the product life cycle, and where production FSAs, such as the possession of intangible skills, are less important than the CSAs of location and energy costs). MNEs in this quadrant generally follow focus strategies of national responsiveness or protected markets. Analogous to cell 2, the possibility exists that strong CSAs could compensate the firm for the absence of strong FSAs.

Cell 4 firms represent inefficient companies lacking any strong CSAs or FSAs. These firms, therefore, should be preparing to restructure or exit. Here we should recognize that, if the firm in question is a subsidiary, effective restructuring may be accomplished by, for example, transferring new FSAs of the parent company to the subsidiary, thus shifting it to quadrant 2.

In the discussion above, each MNE was considered as a homogeneous entity, consisting of a single strategic business unit (SBU). For example, a position in cell 1 would imply that all operations – in cases of concentrated as well as dispersed configuration – would be characterized by strong CSAs. In practice, of course, a distinction needs to be made between the different SBUs composing the MNE.

In this context, we should also emphasize that in the discussion below the term 'SBU' will not be used to indicate all of the MNE's operations, but only its Canadian operations, which may be affected by free trade. Thus, global differentiation, cost-leadership or segmentation in cell 1 reflects the existence of: (1) world product mandates or globally rationalized Canadian affiliates of foreign MNEs; and (2) the domestic operations of Canadian MNEs characterized by such strategies. Similar comments hold for the focus strategies pursued in cells 2 and 3 of Figure 5.1. A national responsiveness or protected market strategy means that the Canadian operations of an SBU are engaged in this mode of behaviour, which does not necessarily always reflect the strategy of the SBU in all geographic markets.

For example, one SBU, which benefits from strong FSAs and CSAs in its home country, may be forced, say as a result of export restrictions, to set up a small, relatively inefficient operation in a host country. This strategy of national responsiveness may be extremely successful since the new operation will now benefit from location in the host country as the domestic, sheltered producer.

However, in an international context, the operation's FSAs may be weak, as its scale may be highly cost-inefficient. Finally, restructuring and exit in cell 4 again only refer to the Canadian operations of an SBU, and not necessarily to the SBU as a whole.

With free trade, changes in CSAs may lead to changes in the entry barriers associated with a particular operation of an MNE. These entry barriers can be grouped as: economies of scale, capital requirements, switching costs, access to distribution channels, cost disadvantages independent of scale, and government policy (Porter 1980). By affecting entry barriers, free trade may shift SBUs to a different quadrant of Figure 5.1, thus requiring MNEs to adjust their competitive strategy. Conceptually, twelve different shifts could result from bilateral trade liberalization (for example shifts from cell 1 to cells 2, 3 and 4; shifts from cell 2 to cells 1, 3 and 4, etc.). In our view, four of these cases are especially relevant.

In the first two cases, free trade, when it implies the abolition of government protection, leads SBUs to shift on the vertical axis of Figure 5.1. Strong CSAs may suddenly be turned into weak CSAs if government protection was an important source of competitive advantage. Here, the elimination of this entry barrier may severely affect the product market domain of the firm. What does this conceptual shift in Figure 5.1 mean in practice? There are two possibilities. Firms may shift from cell 1 to cell 2 or from cell 3 to cell 4. A shift to cell 2 implies that the SBU may have to reconsider the segment scope of its Canadian operations. The elimination of trade barriers will force it to restructure, typically in the direction of higher specialization and a narrower product market domain. A movement towards cell 4 implies that an SBU, whose competitive advantages were based on government shelter, now becomes subject to market forces, which may initiate exit or force restructuring of the Canadian operations.

In the third and fourth case, trade liberalization generates a shift on the horizontal axis, especially from cell 3 to cell 1, namely if it allows SBUs to take advantage of increased market opportunities, thus stimulating the development of new FSAs. For example, free trade may lead SBUs to benefit from scale economies and learning curve effects, thus strengthening their distinctive competence in reducing costs. Here, a shift is generated from the right-hand side to the left-hand side of Figure 5.1. This shift demonstrates that FSAs and CSAs are interrelated: the strengthening of the FSAs of Canadian operations results from the abolition of shelter (strong CSAs) which benefited foreign, in this case US, rivals.

An application to Canada–US free trade

The competitive strategy framework developed above allows us to conceptualize adjustment decisions in response to bilateral trade liberalization. We shall first study adjustment by Canadian-owned MNEs and, second, adjustment by US subsidiaries in Canada. Much of the previous work on economic adjustment has focused on the macro-economic effects of scale economies and productivity gains.[5] Although these factors are clearly important, strategic management decisions by firms are the basic source of any adjustment to freer trade.

As tariffs and non-tariff barriers are reduced and trade discipline is restored, many of the short-run, fragmented production processes in Canada may become inefficient (shift from top half to lower half of Figure 5.1). Thus, much of the adjustment will take place within industries and within firms as opposed to between industries.[6] In addition, trade liberalization may provide an incentive for SBUs to specialize their production and to increase their scale, so that their products are produced for a much larger market (a shift from quadrant 3 to quadrant 1).

Adjustment by Canadian multinationals

The largest twenty-two Canadian public industrial MNEs have been identified by Rugman and McIlveen (1985) and Rugman (1988e). These twenty-two firms are: Alcan, Northern Telecom, Seagram, John Labatt, Gulf Canada, Noranda, Moore, Abitibi-Price, Nova, MacMillan Bloedel, Domtar, Molson, Consolidated-Bathurst, Ivaco, Varity, AMCA International, Inco, Cominco, Falconbridge, Bombardier, Canfor, and Magna International. Key financial data for these firms can be found in Table 5.1, where the multinationals are ranked by their 1986 sales. These firms are already very active internationally. The five-year average ratio of foreign to total sales is 67 per cent, and 42 per cent of their assets are located outside Canada.[7]

This international orientation has exposed these firms to the exigencies of operating in the global economy. Two factors have led them to develop restructuring strategies to deal with the new highly competitive global economy: (1) the harshness of the 1981–2 recession on resource-based firms;[8] and (2) the rise of US 'administered protection,' broadly defined as the use of countervail, anti-dumping duties and safeguard actions to protect inefficient firms.[9]

To understand the strategic decisions made by these firms in

Table 5.1 Performance of the largest Canadian industrial
multinationals (millions of Canadian dollars)

Firm	1986 Sales	Return on Equity (ROE)	
		1977–86	1982–6
Alcan	8,222	3.4	10.7
Northern Telecom	6,091	18.2	15.7
Seagram	4,618	11.7	11.4
John Labatt	4,253	18.4	16.9
Noranda	3,547	0.1	8.8
Moore	2,919	15.4	16.5
Abitibi-Price	2,764	9.6	14.3
Nova	2,681	10.2	10.9
MacMillan-Bloedel	2,512	4.9	8.9
Domtar	2,327	10.3	12.5
Molson	2,250	12.7	15.1
Consolidated-Bathurst	2,018	10.0	15.1
Ivaco	1,945	5.1	12.1
Varity	1,877	0.7	0.7
AMCA International	1,498	2.9	10.9
Inco	1,452	1.1	4.0
Gulf Canada	1,407	12.1	14.5
Cominco	1,328	0.5	9.4
Falconbridge	1,146	2.1	5.1
Bombardier	1,104	8.8	7.0
Canfor	1,047	2.2	n/a
Magna International	1,028	18.2	20.5
Overall average	2,574	8.0	11.3

Source: Corporate annual reports, *Financial Post 500* (various issues), IMF International
Statistical Yearbook year-end exchange rate.
Notes: ROE is calculated as net income before extraordinary items divided by average
equity. Gulf has been excluded from the totals and averages due to a change of ownership
in 1985.

adjusting to this new trading environment, we will analyse them
in their industry groups and position them in Figure 5.2, based
upon extensive and ongoing process analysis of their core skills.[10]
These twenty-two megafirms can be divided according to their
principal operations into minerals, pulp and paper, distilleries,
high technology, oil and gas, and manufacturing.

The megafirms in the mineral sector are Alcan, Noranda, Inco,
Cominco and Falconbridge. These firms enjoy strong CSAs in
their access to Canada's abundant raw materials and proximity to
the US market. These advantages have been internalized into
FSAs of vertical integration. In addition, most of these firms have
developed skills in the production and marketing of at least one
mineral. Due to the recession and the decline in world mineral
prices, they have tended to emphasize global segmentation
strategies, focusing upon low costs. In addition, they have tried to

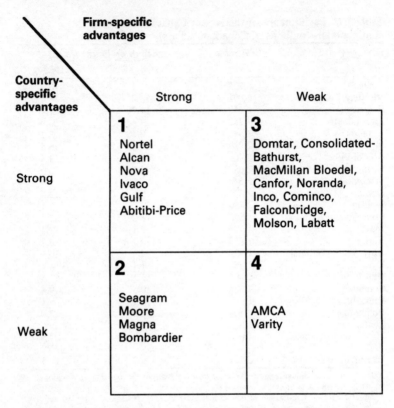

Figure 5.2 The competitive advantage matrix: Canadian MNEs (firms)

move up the value-added chain in processing and manufacturing. These mature resource-based firms have traditionally been situated in cell 1, but their low financial performance, excluding Alcan, would tend to position them in the third quadrant, which implies an erosion of their FSAs.

The pulp and paper sector is populated by mature firms operating within cells 1 and 3. Abitibi-Price, Domtar, and Consolidated-Bathurst are cell 1 firms following primarily low-cost segmentation strategies but expanding their product lines to markets other than their core areas. Some have expanded into other industries such as Domtar into chemicals, Abitibi-Price into up-scale papers and Consolidated-Bathurst into packaging. While MacMillan Bloedel and Canfor are following similar strategies, their consistently poorer competitive performance situates them perhaps closer to cell 3, where they attempt to compete on costs in the low end of the market (in terms of value added).

As with the minerals megafirms, these firms benefit from CSAs in access to Canadian natural resources. They have managed to develop FSAs of a vertically integrated production structure through long-term contracts providing access to forests. The firms in this sector will benefit from the dispute settlement procedures of the Free Trade Agreement.[11] This should insulate these Canadian producers from the abuses of US-administered protection.[12] Thus, in terms of our framework they will move to the left of the horizontal axis of Figure 5.2; secure access to the US market will allow them to develop new FSAs, especially in the area of cost competitiveness.

The distillery and brewery sector consists of John Labatt, Molson Industries and Seagram. These firms have FSAs in marketing their alcohol-based products. Provincial sales and production laws represent a CSA in protection. However, in the case of Molson and Labatt these must be balanced against the inefficient production scale (a weak FSA) forced on the industry, because of interprovincial barriers to trade (leading to the establishment of cost-inefficient breweries in the different Canadian provinces). This inefficiency in manufacturing is only partly compensated for by marketing strengths and brand names, although the latter have permitted some degree of international expansion for Molson and Labatt brewery products. For these products, the two latter firms are largely situated closer to cell 3 than cell 1 and pursue a mixture of national responsiveness and protected market strategies. Thus, Molson and Labatt rely heavily on government shelter. As they operate in a mature industry, each is diversifying. Labatt derives greater revenue from its agri-food SBUs and has been integrating across the US border. Molson has diversified into chemicals and retail merchandising. These SBUs account for over half of the firm's profits. Free trade will have little or no impact on the strategies of these firms. As a result of extensive lobbying activities, Labatt succeeded in exempting the beer industry from the free trade agreement, thus allowing this firm to maintain its protected market strategy and preventing a shift from quadrant 3 to quadrant 4.

As for Seagram, it has also diversified into up-scale premium products. Its strategic equity link (22 per cent ownership) to Du Pont Chemicals has provided the source of capital for this diversification. Most of its operations are already located abroad and its Canadian operations rely primarily upon strong marketing FSAs. Hence, no effect of trade liberalization is anticipated.

Two non-traditional Canadian megafirms are represented by the high-technology innovators Northern Telecom and Moore. The FSAs upon which these firms rely are R&D, marketing, and service adaptability. The CSAs upon which they have built include proximity to the US market and, in the case of Nortel, some government support (merely complementing its strong FSAs). Nortel is a cell 1 firm benefiting from its link to Bell, and its research unit Bell Northern. Moore is a cell 2 firm following a global segmentation strategy. Its emphasis on customization has made its FSAs dominate its CSAs. Both of these firms are well diversified along geographic and product lines, although Northern Telecom is now limiting its segment scope to increase competitiveness. Bilateral trade liberalization will enhance their competitive strengths, through easier access to the US market, thus shifting them even further to the left-hand side of Figure 5.2.

The two megafirms in the oil and gas sector are Nova and Gulf Canada Resources. After a period of reorganization, following its purchase from Chevron by Olympia and York, Gulf now operates as an exploration company. It has sought to diversify geographically into South-east Asia to build on its core FSAs. Nova has diversified into other product areas such as petrochemicals and telecommunications. Both are cell 1 firms situated to benefit from trade liberalization, as a result of stronger market opportunities in the US from which the different SBUs' primary segmentation strategies will profit.

The manufacturing sector consists of five firms in mature industries: Ivaco, Amca, Varity, Magna and Bombardier. The FSAs possessed by these firms consist primarily of marketing skills associated with brand names with a reputation for quality. Nevertheless, cost and price concerns have recently dominated the strategies of these firms. However, some, like Ivaco in steel products and Magna in automotive parts, have managed to move up a value-added chain to service product and geographic market niches.

Amca and Varity are undergoing major restructuring of their operations, dropping core product lines and seeking new ones, such as auto parts and engines for Varity. Varity (previously Massey Ferguson) has therefore moved to the far right of the horizontal axis of Figure 5.2 and is now attempting to develop new distinctive competencies. Bombardier and Magna are successful cell 2 firms emphasizing segmentation strategies based upon marketing FSAs. Ivaco, a world leader in several steel and wire products following a differentiation strategy, is situated in cell 1.

Trade liberalization will not adversely affect any of these three firms.

Adjustment by US subsidiaries in Canada

Canadian industrial policy, dating from John A. Macdonald's National Policy in 1879, has recognized that a protective tariff attracts foreign investment across the border. In the past century foreign manufacturers built plants in Canada to circumvent its high tariffs. As a result, foreign subsidiaries account for over 40 per cent of assets in the manufacturing sector.[13] Today the US share of all foreign investment in Canada is around 76 per cent.[14] Recently US foreign ownership has been falling; as of 1986 it is only 18 per cent of all non-financial corporations.[15]

This section predicts the possible actions of these key US subsidiaries in responding to bilateral trade liberalization. The thirteen largest US industrial subsidiaries in Canada are: GM of Canada, Ford of Canada, Chrysler Canada, Imperial Oil, IBM Canada, Texaco Canada, Mobil Oil Canada, Canadian General Electric, Dow Chemical Canada, Amoco Canada, Du Pont Canada, Suncor Canada and Proctor & Gamble. Financial data on these firms are reported in Table 5.2, where these firms are again ranked by sales.

Table 5.2 Performance of the largest subsidiaries of US multinationals (millions of Canadian dollars)

Subsidiary	1986 Sales	Subsidiary ROE	
		1977–86	1982–6
GM of Canada	18,533	26.5	33.5
Ford of Canada	14,327	9.0	16.1
Chrysler Canada	7,359	65.8	130.9
Imperial Oil	6,964	13.2	9.5
IBM Canada	2,924	25.5	28.8
Texaco Canada	2,719	19.3	17.4
Mobil Oil Canada	1,648	20.6	16.7
CGE	1,642	10.3	9.5
Dow Chemical Canada	1,352	10.0	2.0
Amoco Canada	1,325	18.9	18.7
Du Pont Canada	1,243	12.8	10.8
Suncor	1,150	11.2	5.9
Proctor & Gamble	1,060	17.9	15.1
Overall mean	4,788	16.3	15.3

Sources: Data for the subsidiaries are from the *Financial Post 500*
Notes: ROE is calculated as net income before extraordinary items divided by average equity. Chrysler has been excluded from the overall mean calculations of ROE.

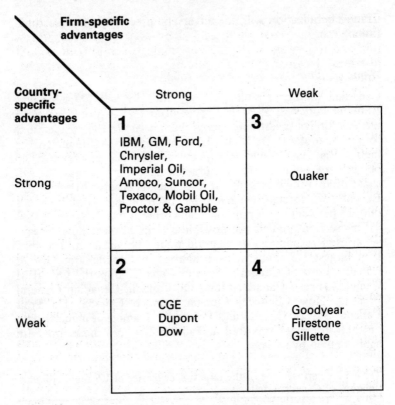

Figure 5.3 The competitive advantage matrix: US subsidiaries (firms)

These thirteen firms can also be positioned according to their FSAs and CSAs and their competitive strategies. However, in doing so it is necessary to distinguish between different types of US subsidiaries. This is done as in Figure 5.3.

Export performance data call into question the view that these firms operate solely as tariff factories (Rugman 1988e).[16] Branch plants whose presence is due solely to the existence of trade barriers, such as tariffs, and which produce on an inefficient scale according to international standards, will always move to cell 4 after trade liberalization. However, even in this case, the availability of strong FSAs of the parent, which can easily be transferred to the subsidiary, may merely lead to reorganization in Canada. In other words, in the short run, such branch plants may move from cell 3 to cell 4, but restructuring guided by the parent may initiate a shift towards quadrant 2 in the long run, typically through granting world product mandates or engaging in global rationalization. Today no causal link exists between tariff protection and foreign ownership; many of these subsidiaries are not just tariff factories relying primarily upon a protected market strategy.

D'Cruz (1986) and D'Cruz and Fleck (1987) have argued that six types of subsidiaries must be distinguished. These range from the importers and local service firms serving only Canada to satellites and branch plants serving North America and, finally, globally rationalized and world product mandates serving a world market.

With trade liberalization, the importers and local service firms will remain intact, as will the globally rationalized and world product mandates. These firms have different levels of managerial autonomy; however they have an economic rationale beyond tariffs, namely to secure the Canadian domestic market through a strategy of national responsiveness in cell 3. The branch plants and satellite operations will more than likely either have to move on to become globally rationalized or obtain world product mandates.[17] In our framework, these subsidiaries would shift from cell 3 to cell 4, because of the elimination of tariff protection. The transfer of FSAs from the parent could then, however, lead to a shift towards quadrant 2. Clearly the process of moving towards global rationalization or obtaining a world product mandate will not be easy. World product mandates will have to be earned by the subsidiary; they will not be routinely granted by the parent. Only where strong CSAs in Canada potentially complement such FSAs will the latter be transferred to the Canadian subsidiary. This would then imply a shift from cell 4 to cell 1, and not cell 2. Only in the case of high exit barriers or distinctive advantages of locating in Canada would such a move be considered by the parent company.

Many American subsidiaries have already begun product diversification to meet the new competitive global trading regime. For example, Du Pont Canada has publicized the reduction of its segment scope to improve productivity and to obtain economies of scale.[18] Interestingly, even with these scale increases they have found that their production flexibility to produce smaller runs has helped them to compete in the United States, even against their parent company.

In practice most of the largest subsidiaries of US MNEs are situated in cell 1. These are led by the 'big three' automobile producers: General Motors, Ford and Chrysler. These firms benefit from the 1965 Canada–US Auto Pact which established a managed trade arrangement for autos and auto parts. Other cell 1 firms building on CSAs particular to Canada and the marketing and production FSAs of their parents are the oil and gas companies: Imperial Oil, Texaco, Mobil Oil, Amoco and Suncor. IBM Canada is also a cell 1 firm. Its parent company has chosen a pattern of international operation that emphasizes local marketing and global rationalization of production.

Proctor & Gamble is another cell 1 firm. The CSAs upon which it builds are access to pulp and paper companies to reduce packaging costs as well as other primary products which are vital inputs into its production process. The firm also builds on its parent's strong FSAs in marketing and established brand names. As tariffs are reduced, intra-firm trade should increase and some rationalization should occur across the border, thus allowing the subsidiary to retain its position in cell 1. Proctor & Gamble has estimated that brands accounting for 45 per cent of its volume can be manuactured in Canada at a cost less than or equal to that in the United States.[19]

Du Pont Canada exemplifies a cell 2 firm. It builds upon strong FSAs in marketing and established brand names. However, with no tariff protection or environmentally based CSAs, it must specialize in areas where it can maintain a strong competitive position based on its FSAs.

Other US subsidiaries positioned in cell 2 are Canadian General Electric (CGE) and Dow Chemical. CGE has already begun to gear up to compete globally by producing inputs for MNEs in Canada doing business abroad. In addition CGE has also allied itself to global markets by acting as a part of a network of the globally rationalized General Electric system. This process has necessitated rationalization of some operations to specialize in certain product lines. With these changes, CGE should be able to continue to exploit the FSAs of its parent and its own ones developed through world product mandates. Dow Chemical Canada also is located in cell 2 based on its parent's FSAs. To move to cell 1, the subsidiary will have to improve on its use of Canada's CSAs.

Cell 3 firms such as Quaker Oats Limited with food processing operations will suffer from the maintenance of agricultural marketing boards raising input prices. These firms, which are faced with suppliers pursuing protected market strategies, will have to restructure to become more globally competitive, or will end up moving to cell 4. Bilateral trade liberalization will prevent them from pursuing protected market strategies themselves.

In cell 4, we would expect to find inefficient 'tariff factories'.

In reality, we see that the few firms which found themselves here after the reduction of trade barriers (and thus their CSAs) have already exited. These include rubber companies Goodyear and Firestone, as well as Gillette.

The analysis here is confirmed by studies for the Economic Council of Canada by Don McFeteridge. He found that foreign-owned subsidiaries adjusted their operations in response to past trade liberalization in the same manner as Canadian firms (Economic Council of Canada 1988). A key conclusion of these studies is that trade liberalization has been associated with the retention rather than the flight of US-owned firms. This implies shifts towards cell 1 and the upper left-hand side of Figure 5.1 as a result of the transfer of new FSAs from the parent company.

Surveys and conclusion

The model and analysis in this chapter is supported by surveys of these key Canadian MNEs and US subsidiaries. In April 1987, a survey of the chief executive officers of these firms was conducted, and the results were reported by Rugman (1988e). A second survey was conducted in the spring of 1988 on the Canadian megafirms. The single most important finding of these surveys is that trade liberalization is welcomed by these firms. Seventy per cent of these megafirms indicated that a Canada–US free trade agreement would be beneficial to them. The basis of support for free trade is rooted in the prevailing belief that the status quo is one of increasing protection in the United States. Sixty-three per cent indicated that the status quo did not benefit them.

On the question of adjustment to a bilateral trade agreement 31 per cent expected to face adjustment costs. However, 80 per cent of the Canadian firms and 94 per cent of the US firms indicate that adjustment assistance would not be required. These results have been confirmed by recent studies by several consulting firms after the signing of the agreement.[20] In the Rugman surveys, 75 per cent of the US firms indicated that they would not close plants in Canada because of the agreement. In fact, 50 per cent forecasted that their investment in Canada would increase between 10 and 20 per cent after five years of a free trade agreement, thus reflecting restructuring efforts to induce shifts towards the left of Figure 5.3.

This chapter has presented a framework to assess the competitive strategies of firms and to analyse their adjustment to the Canada–US Free Trade Agreement. Conceptual and empirical evidence suggest that adjustment is already underway. Both the Canadian MNEs and the US subsidiaries have adapted their competitive strategies to the competitive global trading regime.

Chapter six

Trade and industrial policy in the triad

Introduction: trade policy in the triad

The methods by which nations can shape industrial policy have been at the forefront of recent thinking on global trade relations. The economic success of Japan in the post-war period has led many other nations to attempt to emulate its perceived policy of state support for industry and trade. Even in the United States influential voices have articulated the need for a new view of international economic policy: one in which the United States uses its size to turn the terms of trade in its favour by such means as import protection and export subsidies.[1]

In this chapter we extend our conceptual framework to contrast Japanese and American attempts to formulate and implement such trade-oriented industrial policies. We demonstrate that the Japanese have been successful in reshaping their comparative advantage by the use of effective administrative structures at the national level. We find evidence of a policy structure which enhances the successful implementation of Japanese industrial policies, as centralized policy choices are possible. In the United States and Canada, however, we have observed the recent escalation of decentralized administered protection, rather than the implementation of efficient national trade policies. The nature and extent of this new type of administered protection is considered, and the failure of US and Canadian structure and trade policy is contrasted with the Japanese experience.

Examples and case histories are used, such as American attempts to protect the steel, textile, agricultural and semiconductor industries and the Japanese policies to promote exports of autos, consumer electronics and related high-technology products. The existence of transaction costs in the execution of US trade policy in these areas is noted and contrasted with the methods by which Japan has dealt with the costs of policy administration.

Then, the conclusions resulting from the US–Japan comparison are linked to the experience of trade and industrial policy in the EC.

Implications are considered for both trade policy and the strategic planning of corporations. Finally, the interaction of such business–government relations is examined and lessons are drawn out for the formulation of trade policy in other countries.

The assessment of international trade strategies

The new theoretical framework developed in this book can be extended to allow the analysis of trade policies of different nations and to contrast their distinctive characteristics. Figure 6.1 is a further conceptual assessment of the international trade policies of governments according to their free trade or non-free trade orientation and the perceived degree of their success. The horizontal axis deals with the nature of trade policy and the vertical axis with the 'perceived' outcomes of these policies.

A free trade policy means that government aims to have the international flows in goods and services determined by the economic principles of comparative advantage. In this situation the nation's 'natural' country-specific advantages (CSAs) will influence trade patterns.[2]

With a non-free trade orientation the government shapes comparative advantage in its favour, or at least attempts to do so. It can do this by shifting its terms of trade (if it is a powerful country like Japan or the United States). In this case artificial advantages are created in favour of national firms, which gives them a competitive edge *vis-à-vis* foreign rivals. To some extent every country in the world grants certain trading advantages to domestic firms. Methods include special export-financing arrangements, tax rebates, preferential government procurement and so on.

In Figure 6.1 it is the degree of government support that matters. The main question is whether government has a strongly interventionist policy to guide and direct international trade or chooses to let the market system determine trade flows.

Turning to the vertical axis, the issue of policy effectiveness is a complex one. The concept of effectiveness used here is the perception of trade policy success, which is a normative assessment. This approach can be contrasted to the narrower concept of economic efficiency, whereby, from a global perspective, a free trade environment is always the most efficient (first best). Also in terms of economic efficiency, from a national perspective, it may be efficient to pursue a non-free trade policy in particular cases,

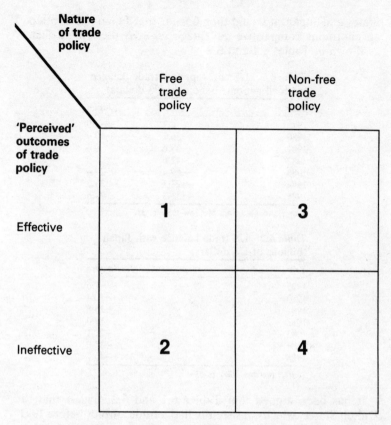

Figure 6.1 Assessing international trade policies

such as (1) the monopoly tariff case; (2) the externalities and market imperfections case; (3) the infant industry protection case; (4) the profit shifting case; and (5) the 'compensating for unnatural market imperfections' case. However, in the next section it will be argued that even from a national perspective, such non-free trade policies will only be efficient if specific conditions are fulfilled.

The US trade deficit

The trade balance of a country is often used to assess the effectiveness of a nation's trade policy. If the American and Japanese trade balances (with all nations) and their bilateral balances are used as a proxy for the success of the trade policies of the United

States and Japan, it would then appear that Japan has developed an enormous competitive advantage *vis-à-vis* the United States, as shown in Tables 6.1 and 6.2.

Table 6.1   US and Japanese trade balance (with all nations; billions of US dollars)

Year	US	Japan
1975	2.2	−2.0
1980	−36.2	−10.9
1981	−39.6	8.6
1982	−42.6	6.9
1983	−69.4	20.6
1984	−123.3	33.5
1985	−143.3	39.6

Source: Adapted from McCraw 1986: p. 31.

Table 6.2   US trade balance with Japan (billions of US dollars)

Year	Balance
1975	−1.6
1980	−10.4
1981	−15.8
1982	−17.0
1983	−21.1
1984	−37.0
1985	−40.7

Source: McCraw 1986: p. 33

It has been argued that Tables 6.1 and 6.2 suggest that the United States, which consistently had a trade surplus before 1971, but accumulated high trade deficits in the recent past, now has an ineffective trade policy.[2] In contrast, the Japanese surpluses indicate a highly effective trade policy which has allowed Japanese firms to develop into global competitors to penetrate foreign markets through exports.

The US trade balance is actually influenced by many factors, including tax policies, government spending, social and industrial policies, and macro-economic factors, all of which constitute elements in a nation's set of CSAs. Moreover, the strength of the FSAs of the companies located in the nation and their choices of entry mode in foreign countries also has a profound influence on the trade balance, as does industry structure in general.

Internalization theory suggests that foreign tariff and non-tariff barriers will increase the relative benefits associated with foreign direct investment, as compared with exports.[4] While such effects may influence a nation's trade balance, they can hardly be considered to represent 'good' trade policy. International trade policy alone does not constitute the main determining factor in explaining how trade deficits or surpluses evolve over time, although it may directly influence the export performance of domestic firms and/or the volume of imports from other countries.

Moreover, a nation's trade balance is only one element in its balance of payments. A trade deficit can be compensated by a surplus on the capital account, because of large short- or long-term investment opportunities. Then the trade deficit should not be regarded as the result of an inappropriate trade policy; instead it may reflect macro-economic factors such as changes in currency valuations and real interest rates. Hence, if a non-free trade policy is implemented as a response to the perceived ineffectiveness of a free trade policy signalled by a trade deficit, the result may well be greater economic inefficiency not only from a global point of view, but also from a national one.[5]

A classification of non-free trade policies

It is important to know how free trade and non-free trade policies fit into the framework developed in Chapter 3, where a distinction was made between efficiency and distributional objectives of government (see Figure 3.1). First, it is clear that a free trade policy fits with efficiency objectives. Second, non-free trade policies may serve both efficiency and distributional objectives.

Figure 6.2 is used to suggest that indeed two broad types of non-free trade policies exist, depending upon their 'FSA-developing' or 'sheltering' orientation. An FSA-developing non-free trade policy has as its prime long-run purpose to strengthen the FSAs of the firms involved and to maintain or improve their competitive position *vis-à-vis* foreign rivals on the basis of their economic efficiency: in other words, it serves efficiency objectives. In contrast, a sheltering policy does not aim at stimulating the development of strong FSAs; protection against foreign rivals is granted. This is done, first, where shelter in itself is the ultimate objective (perhaps as a response to lobbying pressures) and, second, when the satisfaction of social goals (such as maintaining inefficient employment levels in declining industries) is of major importance. Hence, in this case distributional objectives are pursued.

Two types of 'tools' can be used to implement either of these non-free trade policies: import-restricting tools and export-promoting ones. Both types may be complementary components of a nation's trade policy. Moreover, short-term import-restricting measures may well have long-term export-promoting conse-

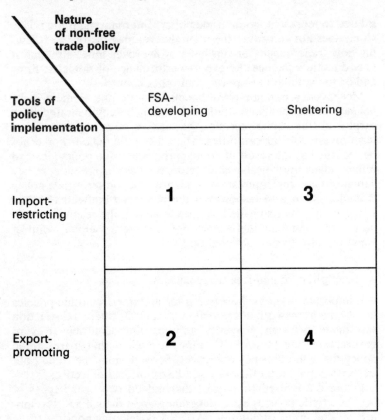

Figure 6.2 A classification of non-free trade policies

quences if domestic firms are able to develop strong FSAs in the absence of foreign competition in the domestic market. This leads to the issue of whether non-free trade policies are efficient from the national point of view.

Sheltering strategies are always inefficient in the long run. They result from the pursuit of distributional objectives and the influence exerted by specific pressure groups on government, reflecting the sensitivity of government decision makers to the demands of clientele groups. High sensitivity to such groups can be explained by the utility-maximizing considerations of politicians and bureaucrats.

In contrast, FSA-developing policies may be efficient if the long-term benefits of government intervention are higher than their short-term costs. Such policies are often difficult to implement successfully.[6] Efficient FSA-developing policies are characterized by selectivity in the choice of firms and industries to which advantages will be granted. Moreover, a policy structure must exist, suitable to implement government policies, without being dominated by the narrow interests of pressure groups. These two elements are especially important in the case of compensating for unnatural market imperfections. Here, a government, which may be in favour of free trade, can adopt a non-free trade policy because of regulations imposed by foreign nations such as trade barriers or export subsidies. As a result, domestic industries face unfair competition from the treasuries of foreign governments.[7] The efficient implementation of such trade remedy laws then requires a policy structure able to discriminate between domestic firms seeking government intervention on the basis of economic efficiency grounds and those merely interested in acquiring shelter. If advantages are granted to domestic firms, the chances of achieving long-run economic efficiency both from a micro-economic and a social point of view, may be increased by imposing performance requirements (such as productivity improvements) and by making government intervention self-liquidating.

Figure 6.3 is useful in predicting the potential effects, whether positive or negative, of FSA-developing and sheltering policies, based upon the degree of globalization of the affected industries. It is hypothesized that an FSA-developing policy may potentially have positive long-run trade balance effects, irrespective of the level of globalization of industries. A lower level of global competition will obviously increase potential effectiveness, since domestic firms will not be confronted with global competitors in the international environment, after having developed strong FSAs. In contrast, a sheltering policy, which is always inefficient, can only be 'effective' in the long run, as measured by the trade balance, in the absence of global competition.

There are eight main reasons why such a policy is bound to fail in the long run, in the presence of global competition. First, if the main competitive advantage of a firm is based on protection rather than overall cost competitiveness, product differentiation or focus advantages, the development of additional inefficiency in resource allocation and production can be expected.[8] Then the firm will be at least partially sheltered from pressures exerted by market forces. As a result the problems of bounded rationality increase; for example, price and quantity signals normally emerging from market competition are distorted, thus influencing important strategic activities such as investment decisions in the sheltered firm. This implies that, in the long run, the chance of

71

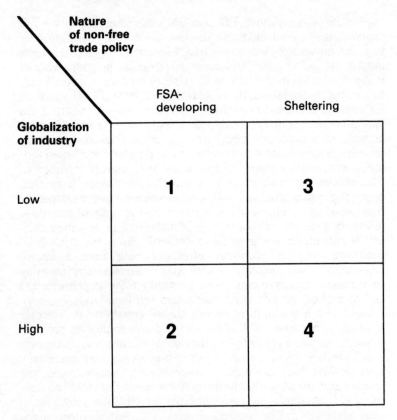

Figure 6.3 The potential effectiveness of non-free trade policies

competing successfully in the international environment with global competitors is reduced. This can lead to negative trade balance effects, in contrast to the case in which government measures would help the firm to develop its FSAs.

Second, if government only grants shelter to firms on the condition that they will comply with social objectives such as maintaining high (inefficient) employment levels and production capacities or increasing income levels in underdeveloped regions, then a new source of micro-economic inefficiency will be created, again with negative long-run trade balance effects. In the context of employment, the danger also exists that labour will attempt to appropriate part of the rents gained through protection, leading to higher costs and reducing the resources available for developing strong FSAs.

Third, if micro-economic inefficiency in resource allocation and production becomes too high as compared with foreign competitors, the shelter provided by governmental protection mechanisms may still be insufficient to guarantee the survival of the firm in the long run, especially if a large part of its production is exported. In this case, exit may become inevitable.

Fourth, the advantages granted by government may depend upon precarious political circumstances such as policy options and budgetary possibilities. The termination of those advantages could then jeopardize the firm's survival and lead to exit, especially if these advantages constituted the firm's main source of strength *vis-à-vis* foreign competition. Such a situation has been characteristic of the shipbuilding and steel industries in different West European countries (for example the UK and Belgium), both in the 1970s and 1980s, where sudden changes in government policy would jeopardize the survival of sheltered firms.

Fifth, if trade barriers are imposed on foreign competitors, this may result in retaliation by foreign governments with negative trade balance outcomes. One example is the retaliation by the EC in March 1984 against US limitations on steel imports. Retaliatory measures were imposed on such goods as chemicals and sporting goods.

Sixth, if the products of sheltered industries (such as steel) are themselves used in downstream global industries (such as automobiles), then the international competitiveness and trade balance performance of the processing industry may be negatively affected. This is especially true if shelter is provided through trade barriers against cheap foreign imports.

Seventh, foreign firms may switch their mode of entry to the domestic markets, for example from exporting to foreign direct investment or joint ventures. An example is the US colour television industry. When threatened by import restrictions in the United States in 1976, Japanese production in the United States represented 25 per cent of US consumption. After the introduction of sheltering measures, Japanese corporations benefited from both the rents accruing to foreign importers and high price–cost margins in the domestic market, thus allowing them to improve their FSAs especially in the area of technology.

Eighth, some forms of shelter such as voluntary restraint agreements (imposed by the foreign country) and orderly marketing agreements (imposed by the home country) confer 'scarcity rents' to foreign producers, i.e. additional resources which can be used to strengthen their existing FSAs. For example, it has been estimated that the voluntary export restraints on the export of

Japanese steel products to the US has increased Japanese steel prices by 10 per cent, representing $200 million a year, i.e. almost half of the Japanese steel industry's investments in R&D.[9] Scarcity rents may thus be very high, especially if domestic and foreign products are imperfect substitutes because of high differentiation. In this case, domestic consumers may even prefer to postpone consumption (through a system of waiting lists) so that the transfer of production to domestic suppliers is reduced.

In addition, if shelter takes the form of quotas or voluntary restraint arrangements, foreign producers may well move up market, supplying only the high-quality varieties of particular products, leaving the low-quality ones to domestic producers. This occurred in the cases of textiles, automobiles and consumer electronics in the United States. After the introduction of voluntary export restraints of cotton textiles from Japan to the US as early as 1956, Japanese producers shifted their production towards synthetic materials and attempted to move towards textile products with a higher value added. The shift was even encouraged by the Japanese government as the quota-granting process penalized Japanese firms with low-price, low-quality products. In the automobile industry, it has been calculated that two-thirds of the price increases resulting from the voluntary export restraints of Japanese automobiles to the United States, in effect during the time period 1980–1, were attributable to quality improvements. In a static sense such quality improvements imply that the welfare losses to American consumers were limited. In a dynamic perspective, however, they imply that Japanese producers engaged in an up-market shift, thus threatening the competitive position of US producers in market segments characterized by high value added and low price elasticity of demand. A similar trend has been observed in the US consumer electronics industry. In addition one result of the orderly marketing agreement introduced in 1977 to restrict Japanese exports of colour receivers was the shift of Japanese firms towards the production of video recorders.

US trade policy

In this section, the recent evolution of American and Japanese trade policies will be contrasted using the theoretical framework developed above. The United States has traditionally pursued a free trade policy. Trade policy implementation was delegated to a technical track by Congress in 1934, in order to shift the responsibility for trade policy measures to a forum in which no interest bias would exist in favour of protectionism.[10] The 1934 Reciprocal

Trade Act allowed the executive branch of government to negotiate reciprocal tariff reductions up to 50 per cent of existing levels
with other nations.

After World War Two, the US free trade policy became even
more predominant. Two major principles of trade policy were
formulated. The first one suggested that international political
interests should dominate trade issues. The second one implied
that free trade would, in the long run, generate the most effective
economic results for the United States (quadrant 1 of Figure 6.1).

There were a number of 'exceptions' to this policy. First, all
presidents since Eisenhower have protected industries with high
lobbying power, such as textiles, steel and footwear. In these
cases, sheltering strategies were implemented, using import-
restricting tools. Second, limited export-promoting incentives
were provided to US firms such as American Export–Import Bank
financing and tax advantages. These partly compensated for sometimes much larger incentives granted by other nations to their
firms. In the latter cases, FSA-developing policies were used.

Within the executive branch, the possibilities of implementing
sheltering policies were limited, as protectionist views in one
department (such as Commerce or Labor) would be confronted
with the free trade preferences of other departments (usually
Treasury and State). The leading role performed by the United
States in the past seven GATT rounds demonstrates that an overall executive branch preference existed for free trade and for the
elimination of international trade barriers.

Today, however, trade policy is no longer insulated against
short-run protectionist tendencies in Congress. The perception by
Congress that free trade policies resulted in major negative effects
for a number of US industries affected by international rivalry (a
perceived shift from quadrant 1 to quadrant 2 in Figure 6.1) led
to the quasi-protectionist Trade Acts of 1974, 1979, 1984 and 1988
(an intended shift to quadrant 3 in Figure 6.1).

The 1974 Act introduced a number of specific non-free trade
elements in US trade law. First, it increased the power of the
International Trade Commission *vis-à-vis* the President, who has
traditionally been in favour of free trade because of broader international diplomatic and political objectives. Second, Congress
limited the power of the President to reduce non-tariff barriers, as
each such agreement would require a majority vote of Congress.

The Trade Act of 1979 and the Trade and Tariff Act of 1984
were designed to change substantially the implementation of US
trade policy. In both cases the intent of Congress was to move
towards quadrant 3 of Figure 6.1, to allow American producers

75

to be protected against alleged illegal dumping and foreign export subsidies. Hence, it was argued that artificial advantages introduced by foreign nations to help their domestic firms should be 'corrected' through the use of an American non-free trade policy in severely affected sectors. The 1979 Trade Act shifted power to administer dumping and countervailing duty cases from the liberal Treasury Department to the Commerce Department. The act also contained restrictions limiting the power of the executive branch in trade policy implementation. The 1984 Act also encouraged the President to engage in retaliation against unfair foreign competition and the International Trade Commission was asked by Congress to use broader criteria when determining the eligibility of an industry for import relief.

The three consecutive changes in US trade policy, as described above, shifted part of the power to implement trade policy from the executive branch to private industry and labour organizations, as it became much easier to demand the implementation of protectionist measures. Some observers would suggest that the intended shift towards quadrant 3 is nothing more than a 'secondary' policy, as free trade goals would still guide US trade policy in many areas.[11] Such a view can be documented by the fact that Presidents Ford, Carter and Reagan rejected the same percentage of 'escape clause' and other general petitions as former presidents, although the number of industries filing petitions for import relief went up from 40 in 1977 to almost 200 in 1984.

In reality, a major shift is presently going on from a free trade policy towards a non-free trade one. Today any US firm or industry can file a petition against alleged unfair foreign imports, and try to obtain countervailing actions. Moreover, as was indicated in Chapter 3, the criteria for determining what constitutes a countervailing foreign subsidy have been broadened with the softwood lumber case of October 1986. As a result, it will become much easier for US firms with weak FSAs to raise artificial entry barriers for their foreign competitors through the use of US-administered protection.

The Omnibus Trade and Competitiveness Act of 1988 has even strengthened this tendency as a result of its emphasis on retaliation and the introduction of new administrative procedures. In particular, if the Special Trade Representative (USTR) finds 'unfair trade' under the new section 301 investigations, retaliation is mandatory (except in a number of specific cases such as those condoned by the GATT). These 'super 301' investigations may lead to a reduction of countervail and anti-dumping actions in the United States as firms may redirect their shelter-based activities towards these 301 investigations. However, this does not imply a decrease of administered protection but only a shift from one type of shelter to another.

From Figure 6.2 the characteristics of the current US non-free trade policy can be identified. The present protectionist policy of the United States, as reflected in the institutional framework available to US producers to petition against alleged 'unfair' imports, is not a 'secondary' policy at all. This would only be implemented in cases of unfair foreign competition when the 'primary' free trade policy led to undesirable outcomes for the nation.

If the present non-free trade policy were really a secondary policy, its orientation would be FSA-developing. In that case alleged foreign subsidies and dumping practices would be compared with 'advantages' given to US producers. It would require selectivity in granting protection, whereby the US government would discriminate between industries and firms that will remain or become internationally competitive in the long run and those that have no future in a more global environment. In this case, the temporary imposition of a CSA (such as protection against unfair imports) would build upon the FSAs of the firms involved or allow them to develop strong FSAs (quadrants 1 and 2 of Figure 6.2). In the case of a sheltering policy however, regulations imposed by government in favour of domestic firms may merely compensate for the absence of strong FSAs.

The non-free trade policy as developed by the United States has a sheltering orientation without any effort at serious selectivity. Little has been done at the federal level to provide special assistance to facilitate American exports, as the United States has provided few tax advantages, little preferential export financing, and only a small number of export subsidies for non-agricultural and non-defence exports. The present emphasis on sheltering through the use of import-restricting policy tools (quadrant 3 of Figure 6.2) raises questions as to its economic efficiency and potential effectiveness to improve the US trade balance in the long run. This issue can be clarified through the use of Figure 6.3.

It has been observed that there is an increased globalization across industries.[12] In this case, the overall position of the United States in Figure 6.3 is located in the fourth quadrant. In terms of Figure 6.1, this would imply that the United States is now shifting to the fourth quadrant where it is pursuing an ineffective non-free trade policy instead of an effective non-free trade policy as prescribed by quadrant three. Although jobs may be saved temporarily in such industries as steel and lumber, at a high cost for the general taxpayer, the trade balance effectiveness of such measures is questionable.[13]

Japanese trade policy

In contrast to the United States, a non-free trade policy was successfully implemented in Japan after World War Two (quadrant 3 of Figure 6.1). In particular, the import of manufactured goods was severely restricted. The Japanese government used an elaborate set of tariffs and non-tariff barriers to limit foreign imports. A policy of selective granting of import licences was even used by the Ministry of International Trade and Industry (MITI) for raw materials. This non-free trade policy primarily served long-term FSA-developing purposes (with some exceptions such as the sheltering policy in the rice sector), with a gradual elimination of import restrictions.

One of the major industries selected for large-scale development by MITI after World War Two was the steel industry. A so-called 'industrial rationalization' strategy was implemented in order to ensure the development of strong FSAs in the protected steel firms.[14] Productivity improvements in the different firms became the main criterion used by MITI to allocate capacity expansion 'rights'. Such an FSA-developing policy was of course conducive to the creation of a strong internationally competitive steel industry, since it stimulated intense domestic competition.

Similarly, Japanese industrial policies in the automobile sector were more 'market promotional' than sheltering oriented.[15] The automobile industry case also demonstrates that MITI could not engage in autonomous central planning. In 1961 MITI made a proposal to organize passenger car manufacturers into three specialized groups (regular passenger cars, minicars and speciality cars), in order to improve scale economies. This proposal was rejected by the industry and domestic competition continued.

In other industries MITI often set target dates when limitations on foreign competition would be abolished. In this way, Japanese firms were stimulated to adopt the most recent technological innovations so as to improve their competitiveness against foreign rivals after the elimination of Japanese trade barriers. Hence, import restrictions were merely a tool to encourage the development of strong FSAs, especially in manufacturing industries where dynamic scale economies were a prerequisite for international competitiveness. During the 1970s and 1980s many of the previously dominant import-restricting tools of the non-free trade strategy have been eliminated. Although non-tariff trade barriers still exist in many sectors, the average tariffs on industrial and mining products entering Japan were lower than American tariffs in 1982 and quantitative restrictions on imports existed for only five manufactured products.[16] The Japanese government has also selectively eliminated import barriers faster than most other developed countries for products in which it chose not to engage in FSA-developing policies.

As to export-promoting tools, these have also been reduced as compared with the 1950s and 1960s, when numerous advantages were granted to Japanese firms with international activities. These included tax advantages, preferential financing, export insurance through MITI, and commercial bank credits at low interest rates. While export incentives remain extremely important, all special tax advantages had shifted to domestic projects by 1975 as the government perceived the existing FSAs of Japanese firms to be strong enough to compete internationally.

A related element is that this FSA-developing policy could be successfully implemented only as a result of technocratic coordination and choice, especially by MITI, which coordinated Japanese trade policies in the post-war period. Japanese trade measures form an integrated part of an FSA-developing industrial policy.[17] MITI does not engage in autonomous centralized trade planning but has a close working relationship with private business (through groups such as Keidanren) and other ministries such as the Ministry of Finance. Selectivity in protection is possible because 'advantages' will only be given to specific firms and industries after extensive consultation with the private sector industrial and trade organizations. This structure is completely different from the US situation, whereby direct lobbying by individual firms or specific interest groups is much stronger.[18] In Figures 6.2 and 6.3, Japanese industries are situated in the first and second quadrants with a clear FSA-developing orientation, which explains the overall effectiveness of Japanese trade policy. The rise of the Japanese computer and semiconductor industry after 1955 is perhaps the classic example of an FSA-developing policy. Here, infant industry protection has led to the development of strong internationally competitive firms.[19]

Trade policy in the EC

The Treaty of Rome includes several articles, especially articles 18, 29 and 110, which suggest that the EC will promote trade liberalization. Nevertheless, in practice this has not stopped the EC from negotiating voluntary export restrictions. Neither has it prevented attempts by the individual EC countries to use national trade protectionism to favour specific sectors. In fact, the European Court of Justice in 1979 advised that the Treaty of Rome should not prevent the EC from conducting policies aimed at regulating rather than liberalizing international trade for specific products.[20]

Furthermore, in many cases, it is unclear how much authority is actually held by the EC itself and how much remains with the member states. This can lead to major problems when conducting international trade negotiations, as was the case with the EC–Japan negotiations in the 1970s.[21] The views of the French and German governments on EC trade policy provide a sample of the large national divergences on this issue within the EC.

The French Government has traditionally been in favour of eliminating intra-EC barriers, including technical standards and procedures for government procurement, but only if accompanied by higher external trade barriers. These barriers should aim to achieve temporary protection for high-technology infant industries. In addition, investment by third countries in the EC should only be encouraged if it initiates the use of new technologies or if it increases employment in Europe. Also advocated are inter-firm cooperation between companies of different member states and EC financing of joint projects.

The German view, in contrast, emphasizes free trade within the EC, but is more sceptical as to the creation of external trade and investment barriers. In addition, public subsidization of joint projects is welcomed only to the extent that it involves basic research which will not distort the functioning of free markets. The erection of investment barriers is also rejected.

In terms of dealing with declining industries such as textiles, the EC has not been very successful. Internally the different member states have developed national protectionist programmes, some of which have been successful (for example in Belgium, The Netherlands and Germany), while others have failed (for example in France, Italy and the United Kingdom). In addition, the EC's external policy has consisted mainly of negotiating limitations on imports, which is the easiest instrument of trade protectionism presently available, but also the most inefficient from an economic point of view.

When analysing trade policy in the EC, it is useful to distinguish three types of measures. First, the measures affecting external trade exclusively; second, trade barriers influencing internal trade; and third, industrial policy measures introduced by the EC or individual member states aimed at affecting international trade patterns.

The first category of measures includes the common customs tariff, which had an average level of 7.5 per cent in 1987 and only applies in full to a limited number of countries (including Communist countries, Australia, Japan, New Zealand, North America and South Africa).

Apart from the traditional escape clause, anti-dumping and countervail actions, the number of voluntary export restrictions (VERs) in Europe has risen substantially. The first VER negotiated by the EC Commission and a third country, was the 1975 VER of steel by Japanese producers. This was extended to several other countries, including Brazil.[22] In addition, several VERs negotiated by single member states exist, especially against Japan (for example for cars, television sets and video cassette recorders). Other countries that have been affected include Brazil, South Korea, Taiwan and some East European countries.

In terms of internal barriers to trade, the most visible internal barrier is provided by Article 115 of the Treaty of Rome. This Article allows a member state to exclude imports of particular goods from other members if import restrictions for these goods were already imposed on third countries. Thereby, 'trade deflection' can be eliminated. During the period 1975–80, a total of 360 applications were approved for France (out of 404), 86 for the UK (out of 201), 95 for Italy (out of 178) and 23 for Germany (out of 23).[23]

In more general terms, the EC Commission distinguishes four categories of internal barriers: (1) general barriers and constraints (such as national preference and legal uncertainty); (2) frontier barriers (such as customs procedures); (3) rules concerning technical safety and public health; (4) other barriers and constraints (such as discriminatory tax and pricing regulations). In the single market of 1992 the bulk of these internal barriers should be eliminated.

Finally, industrial policy is still to a large extent a national issue, as it is not explicitly dealt with in the Treaty of Rome. Article 92 only forbids the use of subsidies that could distort competition. In practice, several national subsidization programmes obviously exist, as in the steel and shipbuilding sectors. Some of these are considered not to be inconsistent with the idea of a Common Market. In addition, the Commission may authorize government support programmes to the extent that advantages to the Community compensate for distortions of competition. Since 1983 the

Commission has become much stricter in trying to eliminate subsidy programmes for which no prior approval had been given.

The main issue is whether the EC has been characterized by an increase in protectionism *vis-à-vis* other triad countries, or third countries in general. Recent developments in policies concerning Japan provide useful insights into this question. It is helpful to compare the bilateral trade balance between the EC and Japan, as was done before for the United States and Japan (see Table 6.3).

Table 6.3 EEC trade balance with Japan (billions of US dollars)

Year	Trade balance
1980	−13.0
1981	−12.9
1982	−12.9
1983	−13.1
1984	−13.5
1985	−14.6

Source: Curzon and Curzon 1987

Although the trade balance with Japan has been consistently negative, it should be emphasized that the EC had a surplus on the current account from 1983 to 1987. In other words, Japan cannot be blamed for 'creating' a deficit with the EC, in contrast to the US–Japan situation. Nevertheless, Curzon and Curzon (1987) have described how the EC has attempted to shelter several industries from Japanese competition through VERs. They have also demonstrated the failure of these policies, as VERs for particular categories of goods appear to stimulate Japanese exports of other types of goods.

The main advantage of VERs is that no concessions have to be made to the affected trade partners, whereas such measures would be required under the GATT escape clause. In effect VERs finesse GATT procedures. Sixty-eight publicly known export-restraint arrangements were in operation in 1986–7 protecting the whole EC market (Kostecki 1987). These include shelter for textiles, steel, machine tools, automobiles, motorcycles, light commercial vehicles and forklift trucks, colour television sets, video cassette recorders and several agricultural products. In addition, many VERs exist at the national level in the individual EC countries (for example television sets in the United Kingdom, stainless steel furniture in West Germany.)

Finally, it should be noted, as in the Appendix to Chapter 4, that the EC is now being characterized by a tendency, similar to the one we have documented for the United States, to use anti-dumping and countervail actions to protect European producers against market forces.[24] The EC has already amended their trade remedy law procedures and used them aggressively against Japanese products such as excavators, printers and electronic type-writers. Dumping margins are calculated in an arbitrary manner and have ranged between 30 and 70 per cent. Multinationals such as Philips have shown a tendency to use anti-dumping procedures against competitors from the triad nations, especially Japan.

In terms of the conceptual framework developed above, the EC is primarily located in quadrant 1 of Figure 6.1. The primary policy of the Commissioners of the EC is one whereby free trade is perceived as beneficial for the Community as a whole in the long run. However, such a policy is often considered to be ineffective in declining industries and high-technology sectors. In old sectors such as steel and shipbuilding, the sheltering policies of national governments have prevented the Commission from pursuing an FSA-developing policy, thus putting the EC in quadrant 4 instead of quadrant 3 of Figure 6.1 and on the sheltering side of Figure 6.2. The VERs against Japan are also a clear indication of shelter-ing policies. However, in the long run it can be expected that the EC will move towards quadrant 1 of Figure 6.1, especially with the creation of a true European market which aims at creating different effects starting in 1992.[25] These effects will include a fuller exploitation of rationalization within firms and prices closer to production costs, industrial adjustments as a result of a fuller play of national comparative advantages, and an increase of inno-vative activity as a result of a more dynamic internal market. The ways in which this more integrated internal market will impact upon the external policies of the EC is not clear yet, but it can be hoped that it would also result in a more liberal view of global trading patterns.

Trade policy for the NICs

The lessons for the newly industrialized countries (NICs) from the models developed here are to beware of the difficulties of policy implementation. The NICs like South Korea, Taiwan, Hong Kong, and Singapore are relatively small open trading econ-omies. They do not have the large internal markets of either Japan or the United States, so a policy of export promotion is required. However, due to the GATT rules, direct export sub-sidies and infant industry protection by the NICs are dangerous policies to pursue. Therefore, the NICs must accept the discipline of operating in principle a free trade policy in quadrant 1 of Figure 6.1, and be careful not to become trapped with the ineffective trade policy outcome of quadrant 2. Another small open economy, Canada, has been in pursuit of this type of open trade policy in recent years.

The NICs, like Canada, can achieve specific trade objectives in selected industries, by operating in quadrant 2 of Figure 6.2. This is an FSA-developing export promotion policy. This issue is developed further in Chapters 8 and 9 on industrial policy in a small open economy. Then if NIC exports are in global industries, they will be equipped to survive in quadrant 2 of Figure 6.3. All of this is easier said than done; but the implementation of successful trade policies for small economies can come as a result of understanding the policies of the triad powers: Japan, the United States and the EC.

Conclusion

What are the implications of the above analysis? The first implication is that the trade balance is not a good indicator of economic efficiency. For example, the United States should not attempt to redesign its policy towards a non-free trade orientation. The administrative heritage of public policy structures and private sector views on the role of government is not conducive to the successful implementation of a Japanese-style centrally coordinated non-free trade strategy. Instead, selectivity is required. Non-free trade policy should only be conducted where it is clear that free trade policies have failed (perhaps because of protectionism of other countries). A non-free trade policy should remain a secondary option and if it is pursued, it should be a micro-efficiency-oriented one. Protection should not be granted to industries whose survival may become completely dependent upon shelter.

The main problem associated with the present system of decentralized administrative protection, especially as practised in the United States, is that it provides shelter. It does not permit discrimination between protecting potential growth sectors and sunset industries that face an inevitable decline because of weakening FSAs. The escalating number of countervailing duty and anti-dumping cases suggests that a non-free trade policy has become the new trade orientation of the United States. In turn these non-tariff barriers to trade which are preventing foreign entry to the US market would explain the enormous influx of foreign direct investment into the United States, as described in Chapters 7 and 8.

The EC is faced with a particular problem when attempting to implement free trade policies, namely, the protectionist attitudes of its member states. The VERs against Japan are a clear example of such sheltering behaviour, aimed at protecting inefficient European industries. Nevertheless, the creation of Europe '1992' is a clear movement in the direction of liberal trade policies in Europe, as it implies the elimination of internal trade barriers. The main question is whether this internal movement will spill over to the EC's external trade policy.

In any case, an important result from the more integrated EC market will inevitably be an increase in the economic power of the EC, thus making the concept of triad power even more relevant. The implications of this for the NICs and for small open economies outside the triad, such as Canada, is that they should actively pursue policies that will generate secure access to at least one of the triad markets. Secure access requires that these countries also pursue free trade in general as a primary policy. The implications of this for the issue of industrial policy are analysed in Chapter 8.

Chapter seven

Globalization and national responsiveness

Corporate strategies for Europe 1992

Previous chapters have demonstrated that US companies can pursue a new type of competitive strategy. By the abusive use of US trade remedy laws, US companies can deny entry to foreign competitors. The US firms who pursue this shelter-based strategy are helping to erect new types of non-tariff barriers to trade since the administration of US trade laws is biased in their favour. Other triad powers are aware of this new form of US process protectionism.

Small nations, like Canada, are scrambling to ensure access to one of the triad markets before global trade wars break out. The MNEs of these nations are key players in offsetting the worst abuses of US trade laws. The perceived increase in US protectionism now raises fears in these smaller nations, and for their MNEs, that Europe may retaliate and attempt to close its markets as it moves towards 1992. This issue of potential loss of market access to Europe will now be examined.

The rationale for the movement towards a single market by 1992 for the twelve members of the EC is being articulated in a large and growing literature. Studies commissioned by the EC have helped to create a favourable climate of opinion in support of the elimination of all remaining barriers to the free movement of goods, services, capital and labour.[1] In this environment of planned trade liberalization and standardization of regulatory and fiscal practices, corporations react by the design and implementation of appropriate strategies. Here the focus will be upon the competitive strategies of non-European corporations, particularly multinationals from Canada. Conceptually, the impact of Europe 1992 on different industries and even on indvidual firms, can be analysed through the use of Figure. 7.1.[2]

The horizontal axis measures the need for regionalism. Com-

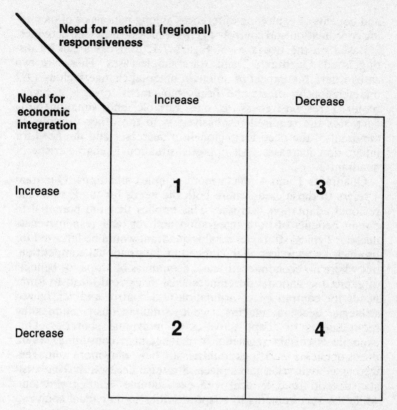

Figure 7.1 The impact of Europe 1992 on corporate strategy

panies need to be responsive to consumer tastes and government regulations in the relevant area of Europe. Regionalism means that activities are adapted both in terms of content and process to local conditions. It is a type of 'national responsiveness'.[3] This may imply a geographical dispersion of activities or a decentralization of coordination and control for individual firms. The single market of 1992 can lead to (conceptually) either an increase or a decrease (or status quo) in the need for regionalism. The vertical axis allows an analysis of the need for integration, frequently referred to as globalization. Benefits of integration are defined as economies of scale captured as a result of centralizing specific activities in the vertical chain in locations with the strongest perceived country-specific advantages, benefits of scope (as a result of the transfer of know-how across borders at low marginal cost), and benefits of exploiting differences among nations or of increasing coordination and control of geographically dispersed activities.

Based on the two axes of Figure 7.1, four cases can be distinguished. Quadrants 2 and 3 are simple cases. These are two cases where the impact of an environmental change such as 1992 unambiguously affects the firm's movement towards a higher required responsiveness to one variable and simultaneously decreases the required responsiveness to the other variable. In quadrant 3, the need for regionalism decreases and the need for integration increases. An opposite situation is characteristic of quadrant 2.

Quadrants 1 and 4 reflect more complex situations. Quadrant 4 refers to those cases where both the needs for integration and regional adaptation decrease. This implies that the potential to obtain benefits of both integration and regional responsiveness decline. Typical strategies for this quadrant would be followed for products and services characterized by international competition, but where no economies of scale, economics of scope, or benefits of exploiting national differences exist. This could lead to lower needs for centralized co-ordination and control and centralized strategic decision making, while simultaneously eliminating requirements to adapt activities to individual countries. One example is certain segments of management consulting, where needs of clients in various countries are becoming more homogenized as globalization takes place. Strategic decision making must stay decentralized to deal with each unique strategic problem, while the requirements to adapt activities to individual countries are being reduced.

Finally, in quadrant 1, the needs for both integration and regionalism increase, implying that different activities in the vertical chain are faced with opposite tendencies, for example a higher need for integration in production, along with higher requirements for regional adaptations in marketing. This is the most challenging quadrant and one where many successful globally adaptive MNEs must perform. Using this framework, we can analyse the impact of 1992 on different industries and firms located both inside and outside the EC (especially third country exporters).

The key proposition in this chapter is that 1992 will put most EC firms in quadrant 3. The harmonization of technical barriers and the reduction of physical frontiers will limit regionalism in production and marketing. It will be easier for firms to operate successfully in the different national markets. In addition, the new entrepreneurial climate, which now already exists due to the expected liberalization, is creating a tendency towards integration.

Consequently mergers and acquisitions will occur as larger industrial groups are formed in Europe.[4]

An important survey in *Le Monde* (1988) of the top management of Europe's 300 largest corporations has confirmed this tendency towards integration. This survey produced results entirely consistent with cell 3 thinking; the managers anticipate increased integration due to perceived benefits of a large market (49 per cent), strategic partnerships, mergers and takeovers (46 per cent), and scale economies (25 per cent). The managers also expect less shelter for textiles, metal manufacturing and agriculture and the development of more efficient modern industries.

Furthermore, the *Le Monde* survey found that European managers were confident that integration was a viable strategy, in comparison to those of rival MNEs in the triad. Only 9 per cent of the European managers expect US firms to gain from Europe 1992, while 42 per cent of them expect US firms to lose their competitive position. A similar viewpoint is held by European managers about the disadvantages of 1992 for Japanese and Southeast Asia firms.

In contrast, a different picture is characteristic of third country firms (such as Canada), now located outside the EC. Though the absolute information costs will decline, these firms will be confronted with increased information costs *vis-à-vis* insiders. In addition, as relatively larger industrial groups actually emerge in Europe, this will increase entry barriers for third country firms. Consider the issue of distribution switching costs; it can be expected that smaller third country firms will find it more difficult to penetrate EC markets if confronted with distribution networks that are integrated to a greater extent with large European groups.

Thus, this situation will put third country corporations without FDI in the EC primarily in quadrant 2. They will find it more difficult to compete on scale economies as the integration option is already being undertaken by rival firms in the EC. They will now need to be more responsive to the specific requirements of the EC market. This constitutes an important problem for exporters from nations such as Canada. They will be confronted with higher marketing costs when exporting to the EC. They will possibly have to consider niche strategies. Only through immediate FDI or strategic partnerships can secure access to EC markets be guaranteed.

This conclusion is in line with the results of a recent study conducted with eighty senior business executives, forty 'insiders' and forty 'outsiders' to the EC. The insiders consider the strengthening of distribution and sales networks to be the major strategic

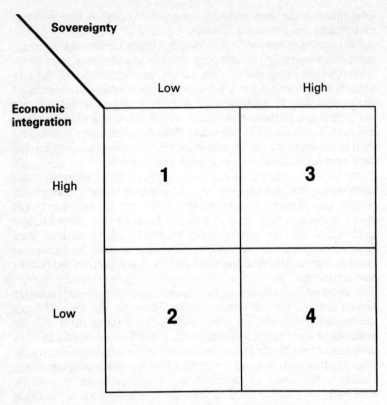

Figure 7.2 The globalization matrix

marketing adjustment that will be faced by their firms. In contrast the main challenges identified by the outsiders consist of creating presence through acquisitions and alliances.[5]

The significance of sovereignty and integration

Many of the issues developed in the book so far can be clarified by reference to the globalization matrix, as shown in Figure 7.2. This figure allows us to classify all nations according to: (1) the degree to which they show economic interdependence with other nations; and (2) the degree to which they are able to determine for themselves their social, cultural and political destiny. The former element could be considered as the level of economic integration, the latter as sovereignty.

On the vertical axis of Figure 7.2 is the degree of economic integration. Towards the top part of this axis there exist strong economic linkages among different countries resulting from corporate strategies such as vertical integration, global rationalization and intra-firm trade in general.

On the horizontal axis is measured the degree of sovereignty kept by each nation regardless of the level of trade and intra-firm linkages on an international level. This sovereignty depends upon the extent to which firms are (or can be made) nationally responsive to the host nations in which they operate. This is partly a political axis. To the right, the degree of sovereignty increases such that MNEs and other corporations wishing to be successful in marketing to the host nation must adapt their products and services to domestic regulations and local community tastes.

Post-war Canadian economic history can be summarized in this globalization matrix. Until the 1960s, Canada was perceived to be in cell 2. The economy was resource-based with relatively small firms and had a large degree of foreign ownership, especially branch plants lacking economies of scale and mainly producing for the domestic market. Furthermore, the mainly American multinationals were rather insensitive to host country attributes and lacked national responsiveness.[6] This is the cell which led to the development of Canadian economic nationalism, whose main proponents, Walter Gordon and currently Mel Hurtig, fear a country dominated both economically and politically by its southern neighbour. In reality, Canada in the post-World War Two period was clearly in cell 4 with strongly interventionist government policies, for example in the fields of regional development and social assistance programmes. This issue will be discussed further in Chapter 8.

In the 1970s Canada was perceived to move to cell 1. It became apparent that more value added was required in the resource industries. There were increased pressures of global competition, so scale economies were required and hence increased specialization, exports and imports. Many economists and other Canadian thinkers believe that this is where Canada would be under free trade; enjoying scale economies and strong economic linkages with other nations, especially the US, the latter element resulting in a lack of Canadian sovereignty.

In reality, Canada today has moved from cell 4 towards cell 3. Firstly, Canada now has strong multinationals of its own. All of the Canadian-owned multinationals are obviously nationally responsive to their home country. In addition, most US multinationals in Canada have now become nationally responsive. For example, the auto companies, IBM Canada, Du Pont Canada, and so on, are all keenly aware of the existence of Canadian sovereignty and they perform within the framework of autonomous Canadian regulations. In other words, sovereignty has certainly not decreased since the beginning of the 1970s.

This matrix demonstrates the myth of the opponents of free trade. They are either old-fashioned cell 2 thinkers advocating protectionism or they understand cell 1 but not cell 3. Free trade certainly moves Canada up the vertical axis; there is a recognition of the high degree of bilateral economic integration in the Free Trade Agreement and this is supposed to become even stronger. But free trade is not just about economics; it is also about politics. The horizontal axis captures this. The Free Trade Agreement exempted all key cultural, agricultural, social services and educational sectors, to the extent that Canadian sovereignty is clearly retained.[7] It is a cell 3 agreement, not one on the left-hand side.

Adding to the plausibility of the globalization matrix in a Canadian context is the knowledge that cell 3 is where the firms (both Canadian multinationals and foreign subsidiaries) must be to compete in the big leagues of the global economy. This point will be developed further in Chapter 8 on industrial policy. Virtually all efficient modern multinationals are characterized by strong intrafirm trade and global integration but also by strategies of national responsiveness to their host nations. This holds for the Japanese, the European, the American and the Canadian multinationals. Today companies need to adapt their product lines to the tastes of individual countries; there are few purely standardized products. Even when commoditization occurs, as in some resource-based products, it is still necessary to be adaptive to host country regulations and aspirations. The days of the 'ugly American' or 'ugly Japanese' multinational are over; today national responsiveness is just as important as, for example, economies of scale.

The critics of the Free Trade Agreement should at least admit to the intellectual reality of the existence of cell 3. Thus, it is conceivable that free trade can lead to greater economic integration, but it can also lead to greater independence, for example, in terms of resources available for the pursuit of national objectives. Integration and sovereignty are trade-offs only in cell 1; in cell 3 they are complements.

The business community in Canada, by and large, already recognizes the existence of cell 3. This is due to its practical experience of triad power and global competition, embodied in highly efficient rival multinationals. It is only old-fashioned nationalists, who have ignored business, that still persist in cell 1 thinking and nothing else. Calls for an industrial policy that would severely restrict corporate entrepreneurship are based on the perception that Canada should move from its alleged position in cell 1 or 2 to cell 4.

Cell 2 thinkers do not recognize the realities of increasing economic integration in the world economy. They believe that the Free Trade Agreement will decrease Canadian sovereignty, while not even bringing any benefits of stronger economic integration; their main concern is the exit of alleged inefficient branch plants from Canada. In contrast, cell 1 thinkers recognize that free trade would speed up economic integration, but they fear an increasing dominance of the Canadian economy by US MNEs and exporters. But they forget about the existence of strong Canadian-based MNEs and strategies of national responsiveness by US corporations. They also neglect the fact that the Canadian government remains sovereign, for example, in terms of industrial policy. This last point is elaborated in the next chapter. The modern Canadian nationalist should discard such outdated thinking, and must recognize the existence of cell 3. Both companies and small open countries need to adopt cell 3 philosophies to succeed in today's complex world.

Investment and the Free Trade Agreement

The text of the Canada–United States Free Trade Agreement contains many important provisions that will have an influence upon trade policy and investment decisions and patterns. The focus on national treatment in its investment provisions warrants a detailed examination. The agreement, of course, has nothing to say about financial capital flows between the United States and Canada. These are determined by interest rate differentials on the basis of market forces operating in the money and foreign exchange markets. There are no effective regulations affecting such bilateral portfolio investments and none are contemplated in the Agreement. Instead, all the discussion of international investment in the Agreement is related to direct investment, i.e. equity investment undertaken by corporations, especially MNEs.

The objective of the Canada–United States Free Trade Agreement was to secure access to the US market for Canadian trade and investment. While much of the legal, political and economic analysis of the Agreement has focused upon security of access for Canada's exports, very little attention has been paid to secure access for Canadian direct investment. Yet, the investment chapter of the agreement is potentially of greater value to Canadians than Americans.

The reason is that today the great majority of international trade is organized and conducted by large MNEs, frequently within the firm. In fact, as much as 70 per cent of all US–Canadian trade is intra-firm. This is a comprehensible number when it is recalled that about 30 per cent of all bilateral trade is due to the intra-firm trade conducted by the three US auto makers within the terms of the Auto Pact.[8]

The investment chapter of the Free Trade Agreement sets an important example for international commercial relationships. As is well known by now, but perhaps not well understood, the Free Trade Agreement enshrines the principle of national treatment for direct investment in both countries. National treatment means that regulations that discriminate against foreign investors are not to be allowed. Instead, American investment in Canada and Canadian investment in the United States are to be treated no less favourably than domestic investment in each country. This will help business efficiency and sustain a movement up the vertical axis of Figure 7.1. The national treatment provision covers the establishment, acquisition, conduct and operation, and sale of business enterprises.

It should be noted that national treatment does not mean that US and Canadian regulations need to be harmonized. For example, on page 195 of the Agreement it is stated that national treatment 'is not an obligation to harmonize'. Canada can have different regulations and standards from those of the United States. National treatment requires that the providers of goods or services in Canada not be discriminated against because they are Americans or Canadians. Therefore, there can be different regulations and standards for an American company operating in Canada compared to one operating in the United States.

In order to exercise its sovereignty, Canada can apply tighter tax and competition policies than the United States, and Canada can design whatever policies it wants in regards to health, social and educational programmes. They just need to be applied equally to Canadian-owned and US-owned firms in Canada. For example, the rules must be equivalent for the management of Canadian-owned and US-owned day care centres in Canada. But Canada can have a different regime and set of standards from those that the United States may establish. Even if the United States has no standards and uses market forces, national treatment still permits Canada to have whatever regulations it wishes, provided they are applied in a non-discriminatory manner.

Canada can even have an active industrial policy, if such an option is deemed to be desirable. The structure required is discussed in Chapter 8. However, due to the decentralized nature of political power in Canada any type of industrial policy pursuing distributional objectives is doomed to end up supporting declining sectors (sheltering policy) rather than picking the winners as the (FSA-developing) Japanese system has permitted. Proponents of a distribution-oriented industrial policy ignore the success of Canadian-owned MNEs which are in mature and resource-based industries. These megafirms have already developed managerial-based FSAs and their successful competitive strategies would only be hindered by government intervention in the pursuit of distributional objectives. A similar argument holds for small and medium-sized firms with successful niches; these companies do not require shelter.

In addition to maintaining Canadian sovereignty in sensitive areas, several key sectors were explicitly exempted from the national treatment provisions of the Free Trade Agreement. These include: culture, communications, transportation, oil and gas, uranium, crown corporations and agricultural support programmes. Hence, adjustment costs for the Canadian economy will be limited.

The current nature of the Investment Canada Act is retained, i.e. Canada retains the right to a screening agency. The threshold level for review of foreign (i.e. US) acquisitions will eventually rise to $150 million, which will still cover all substantial foreign investments. While the review of US indirect acquisitions will be terminated, most other review provisions of the Investment Canada Act are 'grandfathered' (i.e. maintained in force). For example, Canada can still negotiate with US multinationals about research and development, technology transfer requirements, world product mandates and employment. Only performance requirements affecting local content and import substitution have been prohibited, but these were subject to challenge under GATT in any case. In fact, local sourcing has already been found to violate GATT, and been abandoned by the Investment Canada agency.

It is difficult to understand how the retention of a formal screening process can be interpreted as a sell-out of Canadian sovereignty. The opposite is the case; Canada is the big winner on investment. Canada gave up very little on foreign investment controls in Canada but it kept open the door into the United States for Canadian-owned investment. The Free Trade Agreement establishes national treatment, which the United States already has, but grandfathers Canada's current screening agency. Since the United States only regulated foreign investment in an informal, rather than a formal manner, Canada will be the only nation to be exempted from any future American screening agency.

This issue is, of course, a little more complicated. While the executive branch of the US government is committed to a policy of national treatment there are growing signs that the issue of foreign ownership of the US economy may well lead the Congress to restrict entry of foreign investment. Such action would not simply be based on concerns for economic sovereignty (which may have been valid in Canada's establishment of the Foreign Investment Review Agency in 1974). Rather, decentralized pressures from individual US corporations and regions, which now influence congressional trade and investment policy, seek to ensure that US protectionism is not circumvented by direct investment substituting for trade.[9]

To summarize, in terms of strict negotiating outcomes it is clear that Canada is the big winner on investment. Canadian investment into the United States is secure at present and for the future. There already exist a few state and federal restrictions on Canadian investment in the United States, for example, in agricultural land, transportation, media and insurance, but these are not significant barriers to Canadian investment. In general, Canadian investment in the United States is not regulated any more than domestic US investment. Now future US investment in Canada will also be subject to national treatment, but most existing Canadian policies used by Investment Canada will be retained.

The grandfathering of current Canadian rights to review inward investment permits Canada to continue to seek undertakings from foreign investors in a wide range of sectors covering culture, agriculture, oil and gas, and transportation. Due to the Agreement, Canada retains the right, as the smaller nation, to exercise its sovereignty through existing programmes to screen US inward investment. The United States, however, has committed itself to an open door policy for Canadian investment.

The foreign ownership issue

Most of the debate in Canada about the implications of the Agreement for direct investment has concentrated upon the issue of US investment in Canada. Due to the public perception of foreign ownership of the Canadian economy, concern has been expressed about threats to Canadian sovereignty by the application of the principle of national treatment enshrined in the Agreement. But concern about foreign ownership, which again reflects thinking on the left-hand side of Figure 7.1, is frequently based on a misperception. The data in Table 7.1 confirm this statement.

Table 7.1 Foreign control of Canadian industry (percentages)

	Non-financial corporations		All manufacturing		Petroleum and coal	
	US	Total foreign	US	Total foreign	US	Total foreign
1970	28.4	37.0	46.0	56.0	77.0	98.7
1971	29.3	37.6	47.0	57.0	79.7	99.0
1972	28.1	36.5	47.1	57.2	77.5	99.1
1973	27.7	36.5	46.0	57.0	74.2	98.9
1974	27.9	36.7	46.0	57.0	72.0	96.0
1975	28.1	35.5	46.0	57.0	71.0	96.0
1976	27.4	34.5	46.0	56.0	69.0	96.0
1977	27.7	34.8	46.6	56.7	70.9	95.3
1978	26.2	33.5	45.0	55.5	65.2	88.2
1979	26.1	33.6	43.2	53.3	58.9	83.0
1980	24.1	31.7	40.5	51.2	57.3	82.1
1981	21.8	29.1	37.9	48.5	52.1	76.2
1982	22.0	29.2	38.7	49.5	53.5	77.6
1983	22.6	29.6	40.5	50.3	55.2	70.0
1984	22.8	29.7	40.8	50.4	54.4	71.0
1985	21.9	29.0	39.8	49.2	39.6	57.4

Source: Statistics Canada 1985 (Tables 1, 4), 1977–84 (Table 4), 1970–76 (Table 3.31).

Data by Statistics Canada in their annual CALURA publications reveal that foreign control of Canadian non-financial corporations fell from 37 per cent in 1970 to 29 per cent in 1985, but much of this is concentrated in the automobile sector. Foreign control of the oil and gas sector fell from 99 per cent in 1980 to 57 per cent in 1986.

But these are the wrong numbers to consider if the argument is made that the Free Trade Agreement will constrain Canadian sovereignty. We must look at the US ownership numbers, which are substantially lower than those for total foreign ownership. Since 1970 the United States has accounted for around 76 per cent of total foreign control. US control of all non-financial corporations is only 22 per cent. To put this another way, nearly 80 per cent of Canada's industry is *not* owned by Americans. Even with more segmented data US control of the manufacturing sector is 39.8 per cent and US control of the oil and gas sector is also about 40 per cent of the total.

While a number of 39.8 per cent for US control of Canadian manufacturing may still seem to be large, what does it really mean? The single most important industry is automobiles, which is virtually entirely foreign-owned and controlled. Indeed, for 1985, the CALURA number for US ownership of transport machinery is 85 per cent. It is also known that fully one-third of all bilateral trade is in the automobile industry. This suggests that most of Canadian manufacturing and certainly the vast majority of Canadian industry is not US-controlled.[10] In other words, there has been a clear move towards the right-hand side of the horizontal axis in Figure 7.1.

Why has there been this decrease of foreign ownership and control of the Canadian economy over the last ten to fifteen years? There is no single explanation, but a combination of factors has led to the maturing of the Canadian economy and the generation of more Canadian-owned corporations and multinational enterprises.[11] Table 7.2 summarizes data on the astonishing increase in Canadian foreign direct investment in the United States, which now stands at $42 billion, compared to a stock of $76 billion for American direct investment in Canada.[12]

Table 7.2 Stocks of foreign direct investment, 1975–88 (millions of Canadian dollars)

	Canadian FDI in the US (1)	US FDI in Canada (2)	(1)/(2)
1975	5,559	29,666	18.7%
1976	6,092	31,917	19.1%
1977	7,116	34,720	20.5%
1978	8,965	38,352	23.4%
1979	12,063	42,775	28.4%
1980	16,386	48,686	33.7%
1981	21,831	52,123	41.9%
1982	23,137	52,640	44.0%
1983	25,516	55,526	46.0%
1984	30,752	60,538	50.8%
1985	35,521	62,350	57.0%
1986	37,836	66,337	57.0%
1987	40,200	72,300	55.6%
1988	42,500	76,300	55.7%
Average rate of increase	18.42%	7.76%	

Source: Data for 1975–82 taken from Rugman (1987b). Data for 1983–8 are the revised figures supplied by Statistics Canada, International and Financial Economics Division.

Over the period from 1975 to 1985 the stock of Canadian direct investment in the United States grew at over 20 per cent a year. This was approximately three times as fast as the growth of US direct investment in Canada. In 1975, the ratio of the stock of Canadian direct investment in the United States to the stock of US investment in Canada was about 19 per cent. By 1985 it was nearly 60 per cent and, if trends over the last decade continue, by the late 1990s there will be as much Canadian direct investment in the United States as there is US direct investment in Canada.

Economic nationalism, free trade and triad power

Opponents of the Free Trade Agreement include economic nationalists and organized labour. The economic nationalists see the investment chapter as a sell-out to the Americans, whom they allege will have greater access to the Canadian economy as the Investment Canada threshold for review is increased to $150 million by 1992. In fact, the vast majority of significant foreign takeovers are greater than this level so that at least 75 per cent of currently reviewable assets will still be subject to review.

Organized labour has another fear – that the Free Trade Agreement will lead to the closing down of American branch plants in Canada and thus to job losses. This fear is unfounded. For reasons explained elsewhere (see Chapter 5), US multinationals will continue to operate in Canada after free trade in order to supply local markets, to retain access to resources and well-trained human capital, and for a variety of related managerial-based strategic reasons governing foreign direct investment decisions.[13]

The logical absurdity of these two viewpoints is apparent. First, the economic nationalists are afraid of more American investment in Canada. They are cell 1 thinkers in Figure 7.2. Second, labour leaders are afraid of American divestment from Canada. They view the bilateral agreement as a cell 2 agreement. The opponents of free trade want to have it both ways. But do they want less American investment in order to increase Canadian sovereignty, or more American investment in order to protect jobs now and in the future?

Here the position of the unions is correct; jobs for Canadians are important. All the research on MNEs indicates that foreign direct investment in Canada provides jobs; the Auto Pact is a prime example. And this leads to an important conclusion. The interests of the unions and the interests of business are the same under free trade. Unions want jobs and business can provide them.

The so-called economic nationalists are fighting the wars of yesterday. Foreign ownership is no longer a concern for Canadians. Today's economic reality is that Canada now has a mature and wealthy society, a stable political system, and an economy which is building up Canadian-owned multinationals at a faster rate than American ones. The Free Trade Agreement will enhance Canadian prosperity and generate the financial resources to maintain and develop Canada's social and cultural programmes.

What does it mean to be a Canadian in an integrated global economy dominated by large multinationals? Are Canadians threatened by foreign ownership of the economy? Will Canadians turn into Americans after the Free Trade Agreement is implemented? Or can the trade and economic aspects of increased integration be separated from the social, cultural and political dimensions which are the touchstones of sovereignty?

Let us briefly reconsider the two positions on this issue of foreign ownership and sovereignty. One group argues that Canadian independence is compromised by American domination of our economy. The Free Trade Agreement is said to open the door even wider to American investment in Canada. The resulting economic dependence will constrain Canada's political sovereignty. In other words, there will be a move towards the left-hand side of Figure 7.2. The second group believes that the performance of capital is more important than its ownership. They see economic benefits stemming from American investment in Canada. Foreign investment creates wealth and jobs, and is good for both business and workers. They believe that Canada has matured as a nation and that foreign ownership does not reduce sovereignty. On the contrary, there will be a move towards cell 3 of Figure 7.2.

Would the perception of American economic domination be diminished by the substitution of Japanese or European products to replace American ones? Is foreign ownership the issue, or American ownership? Should only products made by Canadian-owned firms be consumed? This, of course, is now impossible for a relatively small trading nation in an interdependent global economy. If Canadians want efficient production and consumption, then they are tied into the world economic and trading system.

The emergence of large MNEs has changed the face of international business in the last thirty years. As noted earlier, today some five hundred MNEs control over half of the world's exchange of manufactured goods and services.[14] These large MNES come mainly from Europe, the United States and Japan. Other writers have analysed the significance of these large multinationals and deduced that there is extreme competitive rivalry amongst them. The most influential is business consultant Kenichi Ohmae, whose work on triad power has changed the thinking of many managers (see Ohmae 1985). He sees intense competition between multinationals based in the triad markets of Japan, the United States and the European Community. His vision of the world is realistic. It is an antidote to those who still seem to believe in monopoly capitalism and American hegemony. Today it must be clear that the multinational enterprises of the United States are being challenged by Japanese and European ones. Any perceived rents are being eaten up by the dynamic forces of global competition.

In a world of triad power it is clear to logical thinkers that secure access to the market of one of the triad powers is essential. It does not take much deductive ability to work out why the United States market is at least as attractive to Canadian business than the more distant markets of Europe and Japan. The critics of the Free Trade Agreement need to present a viable alternative and explain how it would work in a world of multinational enterprises and global competition.

Conclusion

Today, within the world economy, triad power predominates. The vast majority of international trade and investment is controlled by multinationals based in the three key seats of economic power: Japan, the United States and the European Community. To be a survivor in today's competitive global marketplace, Canada needs access to the markets of one of these triad powers. Canadians are reaching out to Japan and Europe through the current GATT round, but are unlikely to get very far; indeed they are more likely to be caught in the crossfire of triad trade wars. The Free Trade Agreement secures access for Canada's trade and investment to the only viable triad power open to them – the United States.

Against this background of the realities of global rivalry and competition, the concern over foreign ownership is factually incorrect and economically misconceived. Canada is now a player in the big leagues. Some of Canada's own multinationals already compete in the triad. Other Canadian businesses need access to the US markets in order to gear up for global competition. The path to future prosperity lies in the Free Trade Agreement, especially in its forward-looking investment provisions. All Canadian businesses need immediate and secure access to the US market for trade and investment in order to gear up for the next century of global competition.

101

Chapter eight

An industrial policy for a small open economy

Introduction: trade and industrial policy

In a small open economy like Canada, trade policy and industrial policy are complementary. Industrial policy is defined here as all government measures aimed at improving the economic performance of particular sectors. Typically, in a small open economy many sectors are characterized by either competition from foreign exporters or the presence of foreign MNEs in the domestic market, or by competition from foreign firms in foreign markets.

This definition means that trade policy is an integral component of industrial policy. All trade policy measures related to the industry-specific erection or elimination of trade barriers, and to industry-specific support programmes for domestic firms with exports or operations abroad, constitute part of a small nation's industrial policy. Furthermore, government support and adjustment programmes for domestic industries in the form of tax incentives, production subsidies, cheap loans, etc., may have a substantial impact on trade patterns. They do this by increasing the competitive strengths of firms in selected industries, or by absorbing adjustment costs resulting from the decline of older industries.

Optimal trade and industrial policy in a small open economy

Free trade as an economic policy has been synthesized and defended by Anne Krueger on four grounds. First, it is a single country's welfare-maximizing policy under the conceptual conditions of neo-classical economics. In this type of laissez-faire regime an optimum is generated whereby efficient production and consumption take place simultaneously. This case, however, only holds under restrictive assumptions such as perfect competition in domestic markets for production factors and goods, constant returns to scale, absence of dynamic factors in production and given international prices. An obvious example, where free trade is not optimal for a large country, is the monopoly tariff case, whereby international prices are not given. Second, free trade is a welfare-maximizing set of policies for the global economy. Third, free trade is a comparatively better alternative than interventionist policies. Fourth, free trade is a welfare-maximizing policy for one country, even if the unrealistic assumptions of the first case do not hold (Krueger 1986).

Krueger has demonstrated, building upon the work of generations of world trade economists, that none of the traditional arguments put forward in defence of trade protectionism can unambiguously guarantee a higher welfare in a country than would be the case under free trade (Krueger 1986). Hence, it is not reasonable to attack free trade using the rationale that the restrictive assumptions mentioned above (first case) do not hold when the alternative proposed, i.e. an interventionist trade policy, will only lead to comparatively higher welfare if equally restrictive assumptions hold. Using a comparative institutional view, free trade may then still be an optimum in real world situations (third and fourth cases mentioned above).

While the elimination of trade and investment barriers undoubtedly increases consumer welfare it is not evident that the unilateral decision of a government to have a laissez-faire, laissez-passer industrial policy would lead to similar results. The abolition of restrictions on imports and inward investment is often the result of bilateral and multilateral agreements, leading to strong increases in economic welfare for all nations involved. Industrial policy objectives, then, are best achieved by direct measures rather than by the misuse of trade policy. For example, the direct subsidization of domestic industries is a more appropriate tool to correct domestic market failure than non-tariff barriers and voluntary export restrictions. In terms of policy instruments to be used when stimulating high-technology industries, direct subsidies to domestic R&D are superior to trade barriers against imports of R&D intensive goods. This is because the relationship between R&D inputs and outputs is much stronger than the linkage between the volume of imported high-technology goods and domestic R&D outputs. In R&D, there may not even be a negative relationship at all between high-technology imports and domestic R&D activity in one industry. Here the elimination of trade and investment barriers improves economic efficiency.

The picture is somewhat different, however, for industrial policy in general, especially support of domestic activities and export promotion. Strongly interventionist policies characterize the economic systems of most nations, including industrialized countries (and thus the triad), the NICs and developing countries. For policy relevance, the main question to investigate is not in which special cases governments should intervene, but rather which instruments should be used, or not used, to attain specific industrial policy goals. This requires an understanding of the comparative institutional framework.

While national efficiency goals should be pursued, the outcomes of alternative policies should never be assessed against the hypothetical efficiency outcomes characteristic of neo-classical perfect competition or cases whereby multilateral (global) restraints would be put on the scope of industrial policies. A more realistic framework requires that two conditions be recognized. First, that the activities of most, if not all, industries are presently characterized by some degree of market imperfection, some of which can actually be corrected by government intervention. Second, that most, if not all, governments in the world intervene actively to improve the international competitiveness of their domestic industries.

Building a model of trade and industrial policy

The model of efficient industrial policy in a small open economy to be developed here builds upon three assumptions. First, most industries are characterized by highly imperfect markets, as a result of various factors including scale economies. Second, government is in favour of some form of active industrial policy to promote the country's international competitiveness. Third, in the case of a small open economy, it is impossible to change the terms of trade, as the small open economy enjoys neither purchasing nor selling power over imports or exports. Thus restrictions on the international movement of goods and capital flows should be minimized, especially if the probability of retaliation by larger trading partners is high.

The second assumption involves measures promoting firms engaging in production, marketing and or infrastructure activities in the home country and firms exporting goods to other countries in selected industries. This preference for some type of industrial policy is considered to be given. In addition, it is recognized that a number of industrial policy measures are taken to aid 'losing' companies and sectors. This occurs not merely as a result of lobbying pressures, but because vote-maximizing politicians respond to a preference of society at large for providing 'fair treatment' to certain declining industries.[1] In other words, a perceived collective good is being provided by government when certain firms face a decline because of international competition. It is presumed that similar intervention would not take place if the decline were due to domestic factors.

The main advantage of assumption two is that international competition can be considered as an uncontrollable variable imposing undeserved losses to domestic companies. Hence, industrial policy measures in favour of these sectors cannot be explained merely as the result of the lobbying activities by powerful interest groups. Such measures, however, cannot be defended on efficiency grounds, but a government bias in favour of losers must be recognized by policy analysts.

Once the three assumptions are considered to have any validity, then it is no longer possible to advocate a laissez-faire, laissez-passer industrial policy as a rule of thumb. The activities of bureaucrats and politicians are not primarily guided by efficiency considerations. The reality is that these groups are actively engaged in industrial policy making. Most questions relevant to industrial policy then do not deal with the issue of how much government is needed (although this subject is in itself important) but rather which instruments are most efficient to attain particular goals, given that the 'quantity' of government intervention is more or less fixed.

Furthermore, even if it can be argued that declining industries should not be helped, the main question for policy analysts is often related to the policy instruments to be used to support 'losers'. Consider, for example, the preservation of jobs in declining industries. In this case government support is provided as an insurance to workers, which, in fact, implies the granting of a limited property right in their job. The key issue is whether property rights should be conferred through, for example (1) supporting the declining firm, (2) providing direct compensation to workers or (3) supporting retraining programmes and mobility allowances, which will help workers to find new jobs.

A strategic model of industrial policies

In developing a relevant model of appropriate industrial policies we make two further assumptions. First, the 'level' of government intervention is considered as largely fixed. Second, declining industries faced with strong international competition are helped in order to provide a perceived collective good. Our model identifies the key instruments required to improve the international competitiveness of the nation. Only policies affecting traded sectors in the most efficient way are considered.

The framework developed in Chapters 3 and 6 suggests that non-free trade policies conducted in specific industries should be FSA-developing rather than sheltering. This implies that government support should be (a) granted to the activities with the highest expected dynamic internal and external economies, (b) restricted in time and (c) allocated in an 'objective' way, so as to minimize unintended policy outcomes resulting from pressure groups. If an FSA-developing policy is pursued, it should be recognized that four different options are open to each nation, in order to improve the international competitive position of its industry through a particular 'positioning' *vis-à-vis* foreign countries. These four options are represented in Figure 8.1.

The horizontal axis distinguishes two alternative ways of designing a domestic industrial policy. One possibility is to engage in a reactive mode of behaviour. The main thrust of industrial policy here is to imitate the behaviour of other countries, which are perceived as being effective in securing the competitive position of their industry. The other alternative is to engage in a proactive policy. Here measures are being taken, not merely as a reaction to industrial policies in other countries, but in a more offensive fashion, independently of policies in other countries or through international policy coordination.

The vertical axis distinguishes two different attitudes towards foreign policies, a cooperative attitude and a non-cooperative attitude. The former implies that stable relationships, with increased economic integration, are being pursued. The latter reflects policies which do not attempt to achieve stronger economic integration. On the contrary, other nations are considered as competitors that can be 'beaten' by appropriate government support for domestic industries. Four policy alternatives can now be identified: rational imitation, defensive reaction, selective differentiation and total differentiation.

First, the policy of rational imitation (quadrant 1 in Figure 8.1) is one where government attempts to copy the policies of important trading partners in a cooperative way. The only measures taken are those that will lead to greater economic integration. Thus, the policy content and process prevailing in other countries dictates the format of industrial policy in the nation with a policy of rational imitation.

Second, is a policy of defensive reaction, as shown in the second quadrant in Figure 8.1. Here interventionist policy measures taken

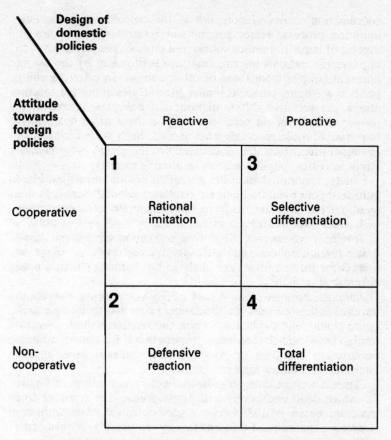

Figure 8.1 The strategic positioning of FSA-developing industrial policies

abroad are again copied, but this does not improve economic integration. On the contrary, industrial policy consists primarily of retaliatory measures at the expense of foreign firms, which include both foreign exporters and foreign MNEs investing in the domestic market.

Third is a policy of selective differentiation (quadrant 3 in Figure 8.1). Here, government attempts to fine tune its policies with those of foreign governments, especially large trading partners. In contrast to a policy of rational imitation, the policy of selective differentiation does not mean the mere copying of foreign policies. Although some degree of harmonization may be sought, this will be realized as a result of international coordination or negotiation, not as the outcome of a domestic imitation process. Here, government retains full autonomy in aspects of industrial policy considered crucial. The objective is to improve the nation's international competitiveness by the use of different policies from those of other nations. In effect, 'niching policies' are being pursued, similar to strategies in private corporations. As selective differentiation is a policy of international cooperation, it should occur primarily in those areas not subject to possible hostile reactions from abroad. Such areas include, for example, support for the educational system, health programmes, R&D activities, public agencies facilitating exports, etc.

Finally, quadrant 4 identifies a total differentiation policy. Here industrial policy is used to create economic self-sufficiency. In this quadrant attempts are made to limit economic interdependence with other nations and a hostile attitude prevails against policies of foreign governments. Therefore retaliation against perceived unfair foreign policies, and attempts to close down the domestic market for foreign firms, are likely to be characteristic of a total differentiation policy.

Although options 2 and 4 may be FSA-developing policies in terms of policy formulation, the danger exists that their implementation would lead to shelter. A non-cooperative attitude towards foreign firms, and governments, implies that trade and investment barriers are being set up which protect domestic firms against international market forces.

Figure 8.1 constitutes an industrial policy application of Figure 7.2 which dealt exclusively with trade policy. The complex free trade agreement of 1988 between Canada and the United States is a clear expression of a willingness by the national governments of both countries to stimulate economic integration. This is achieved by eliminating trade barriers while at the same time maintaining sovereignty not only on political and cultural issues, but also on domestic economic policies.

Our conclusion is that a selective differentiation policy is optimal for Canada, or any other small open economy which is not a member of the triad powers. In general terms, this policy of selective differentiation should recognize several elements.

It is of prime importance to secure easy access to at least one of the triad economies. This can be achieved through a proactive government policy aimed at establishing closer links with the triad power concerned. Another major element is not to fall into the trap of a reactive policy of rational imitation. This would lead the smaller country into becoming a 'satellite' of the larger power. Then the 'asymmetry argument' would hold.

The asymmetry argument states that firms from the smaller country would encounter higher entry barriers when penetrating the triad power's market, whereas corporations from the latter country would consider the smaller nation's market as incremental, requiring only minor increases in, for example, production and marketing efforts. If this argument is correct, and asymmetries do arise in a number of sectors, an industrial policy of selective differentiation requires 'efficient' support programmes, i.e. measures with the largest long-run wealth-creating effects. Such programmes must be aimed primarily at compensating for asymmetries without endangering the cooperative nature of the economic relationships with foreign nations.

Such a policy shifts the focus of government measures from the inefficient sheltering of declining firms towards the development of FSAs aimed at overcoming entry barriers in the foreign market. In other words, CSAs shaped by government through industrial policy complement the FSAs of participating firms instead of being substitutes for them. Furthermore, stronger FSAs may in turn lead to improved CSAs. For example, an important reason for improved CSAs may be that larger markets allow contracting out of activities towards specialized corporations, which become viable only because of the larger market. A more open market accessible to domestic firms provides a more efficient division of activities between firms (in-house production) and markets (contracting out). Such an improved allocation of resources creates a positive external benefit, which is not captured in the decrease of transaction costs for the firms involved.

Apart from bilateral trade liberalization, free trade on a multilateral scale should also be pursued within the framework of a policy of selective differentiation. First, multilateral agreements such as the ones negotiated within the GATT provide a set of 'objective' rules, improving the stability of the international trading regime (although these rules may be subverted, as in the case of US-administered protection). Second, the requirements to comply with the rules of international agreements may reduce the bargaining power of domestic pressure groups seeking shelter from global market pressures.

The option of defensive reaction is always a fallacy for a small open economy. Even if larger trading partners engage in highly protectionist policies, retaliation or the pursuit of identical industrial policies is useless. The relative economic impact on the market of the larger economies will be negligible when compared to the impact of their policies on the small nation's economy. Since the use of a tit-for-tat approach results in an escalation of protectionism and government competition on international markets, this leads to negative effects on the small economy. The government of a small nation should never seek retaliation or the imitation of hostile industrial policies in such areas as investments. On the contrary, it should try to adopt a cooperative attitude and attempt to eliminate the costs of foreign industrial and trade policies through negotiations with larger, non-cooperative trading partners.

Finally, the worst possible option is a policy of total differentiation. Here the government of a small economy pursues self-sufficiency through initiating hostile policies *vis-à-vis* larger trading partners and foreign firms. One of the main results of a total differentiation policy, emphasizing tariff protection, is the creation of 'miniature replicas'.[2] This was characteristic of Canada until World War Two. It was this approach that led to the creation of the Foreign Investments Review Agency (FIRA) following the so-called Gray Report in 1972. The negative effects resulting from FIRA's activities on economic activity in Canada have been described elsewhere.[3] In addition, Canada's National Energy Program, developed after the oil crisis of 1979, led to strong inefficiencies. All these examples of total differentiation policy fail in small open economies like Canada.

Industrial policy, entry barriers and small firms

There is a strong relationship between domestic entrepreneurship and wealth creation. The small entrepreneurial firms of today, especially in traded industries, are the exporters and multinationals of tomorrow. It is not the task of government to pick out winners, but any imperfections in the capital market provide a reason for granting financial incentives through government support programmes. This is especially true when recognizing the asymmetry problem mentioned above, a situation faced by all small open economies.

The asymmetry argument may hold for concentrated industries. Here exporters from a smaller nation find it difficult to penetrate larger foreign markets.[4] In contrast, the exporters from larger countries find it easy to penetrate smaller, incremental markets.

Government may intervene when small firms in a small open economy are confronted with entry barriers when penetrating foreign markets. These barriers include the creation of marketing and distribution networks which require high set-up costs. When the entry barrier is unavailability of capital, because of the risks perceived by private financial institutions, providing cheap loans and interest subsidies may then allow small firms to set up operations abroad. Yet government should not be concerned with picking out winners itself; the support programme should be generally available to all firms fulfilling certain preset criteria (see pp. 114–16). The firms able to use government support as an instrument complementing their FSAs will then be successful in the international marketplace.[5] In other words, the actual market opportunities and threats should be identified and translated into strategic actions by business firms, not by government agencies.

It is self-evident that some limits must be put on the general availability of support programmes. Support should only be granted to firms that require it to penetrate foreign markets. Large firms with international operations should be excluded. It may prove more difficult, however, to exclude smaller firms which are engaged in focus differentiation strategies and which do not face substantial entry barriers. In this case, government support will complement strong FSAs and provide such firms with additional competitive advantages although such firms do not really need this support. It is crucial to limit the availability of support over time, so that firms do not use it as a substitute for the development of strong FSAs.

Industrial policy and innovation

So far we have adopted a static analysis relating government support to small domestic firms with given products or services in order to penetrate foreign markets. In a dynamic analysis, government policy itself may help to alter the structure of products and services provided by domestic firms. Preemptive support policies could be introduced in cases where high and irreversible sunk costs lead to a market structure consisting of only a few firms.[6] Companies missing the first wave of investment in particular technologies may find it unprofitable to enter the market later and compete with established firms. This occurs when an industry or product line experiences high learning curve effects.

There are substantial differences between the traditional infant industry argument and this dynamic internal economies case. The major aims of government policy in the latter case, are to create firms sufficiently large to compete in international oligopolies and to preempt additional foreign entry in the global marketplace. This contrasts with the old view of infant industry protection, whereby domestic market imperfections stimulated government to create support programmes in otherwise internationally competitive markets.

Can government in a small open economy pursue preemptive policies by supporting local industries? Such a policy is bound to fail if tariffs are used. The domestic market is too small to reap the dynamic internal economies hoped for, and retaliation could occur. The use of subsidies is inefficient when similar policies are pursued by foreign governments.

When this last condition holds dynamic internal economies will not be translated into economic rents (since several governments pursuing similar policies create global excess capacity). Hence, only those firms and industries should be supported which also create high dynamic external economies in the form of 'spillover' effects in the domestic economy. Thus government policy should focus primarily on helping firms to raise the value of their human capital and advance their innovation efforts. Hence, there should be an emphasis on investments in intangible assets rather than fixed assets.

Investments in R&D can create substantial national spillover effects, to the extent that they facilitate the innovation process in other firms.[7] Such externalities may take two forms. First, proprietary technological know-how may diffuse towards suppliers, distributors and customers who need to develop a thorough knowledge of the firm's products. Second, in a dynamic perspective, the internal development of human capital within the innovative firm may lead to diffusion when technically skilled employees set up their own entrepreneurial activities or shift to other companies. This has occurred when Northern Telecom's employees have left to found firms such as Mitel.[8]

The level of R&D expenditures expressed as a percentage of GDP is not a good indicator of the level of technologically advanced output in a nation. Higher inputs may simply reflect inefficiency in the process of creating technological know-how; there need not exist a strong connection between inputs and outputs. A small open economy may well benefit from the important presence of subsidiaries of foreign MNEs. Although these subsidiaries may not engage in substantial R&D activities themselves, they still benefit from the strong FSAs of their parent company, which may be technology based; a basic premise of internalization theory. As a small open economy cannot specialize in all new technologies, it may be more efficient to improve the domestic diffusion and transferability of technology. Then technologies developed abroad can be more easily absorbed. Free trade in high-technology goods should be stimulated as much as possible to create spillover effects in the domestic economy, especially if domestic services need to be provided, for example, to service imported high-technology goods. The same argument holds for the establishment of subsidiaries by foreign MNEs in high-technology sectors. Even if no basic R&D is performed, the use and training of a highly specialized labour force may generate important spillover effects for the domestic economy. Selective measures stimulating industrial R&D may be useful for two main reasons. First, the 'success breeds success' hypothesis suggests that the initiator of an innovation can obtain an indefinite competitive advantage over foreign rivals if the existing technological gap is maintained.[9] Second, if it is assumed that government support programmes will be implemented anyway, it is more efficient to support R&D activities with potentially strong spillover effects than, for example, investments in fixed assets. The stimulation of R&D activities shifts the structure of an economy towards production of high-technology goods with high value added, high wages and substantial externalities. Even if no economic rents are obtained by firms in high-technology sectors, because several governments subsidize their domestic companies, the external economies and high value added still remain.

A problem associated with supporting innovative activities is that entry barriers for small open economies in high-technology sectors do not occur only in the innovative R&D activity stage. Entry barriers also occur in the exporting stage, when marketing and distribution channels need to be set up. This leads to three important policy prescriptions. First, the effectiveness of government programmes, in the form of R&D support, may only be successful if complemented by export-promoting policies. Second, free trade with larger countries must be actively promoted to help decrease entry barriers for domestic firms. Third, the technology-stimulating component of an industrial policy should not attempt to consider domestic R&D and technology transfer by MNEs (import of 'foreign' technology) as alternatives, out of which one has to be 'chosen'. Both forms of activities should be enhanced and should be regarded as complements instead of substitutes. However, given the fact that technology transfer by MNEs, through the creation of subsidiaries or licensing agreements, will obviously not be confronted with entry barriers (in the absence of government regulations), the prime emphasis of government support should be on the development of domestic R&D (without thereby being discriminatory *vis-à-vis* the domestic operations of foreign-owned firms).

The issue of industrial targeting

An 'industrial targeting' strategy occurs when government wishes to stimulate the development of domestic multinationals or internationally competitive firms in traded industries with high value added per employee. Industrial targeting of specific sectors, including the selection of firms to benefit from support programmes following preset criteria, is not the same thing as attempting to pick winners. Only if certain targeted sectors consist of just one or a few firms, and support programmes are tailored to the needs of individual firms, does targeting and the selection of winners become almost synonymous. But the degree of selectivity depends upon the industry. Only in cases where high concentration is required to be successful in global markets should targeting of one or a few firms occur. In these rare cases government may then be forced to pick winners.

The implementation of such a strategy constitutes a major problem for countries with a highly decentralized power structure of government. In Canada the different regions, or provinces, must abstain from picking winners. The use of provincial government procurement measures for this purpose would probably be guided by considerations of regional development and employment. Then, a self-defeating bidding process among regions or provinces would be created. This would be accompanied by a politicized support-granting process, which would result in sheltering policies for 'chosen' companies.[10] If selecting winners takes place it should be done at the national level or not at all. Even then, it is important to restrict the selection of perceived winners to concentrated industries that fulfil specific criteria.

Figure 8.2 provides a framework for selecting industries to be targeted. It is based upon two criteria, namely the export potential of the industry and the potential value added per employee in the industry. Within this framework, a highly developed, small open economy should attempt to target industries in the fourth quadrant. These would include traded services, high-technology sectors, and also more mature sectors with high niching potential. Within these industries, however, if high concentration on a global scale can indeed be observed and picking winners seems required, only those firms which already have demonstrated substantial export capabilities, and have a high value added per employee, should be selected, so as to reduce the demand for shelter.

In industries having many suppliers in the global market, government support should accrue to all firms. In an oligopolistic industry characterized by high entry barriers, industrial policy can

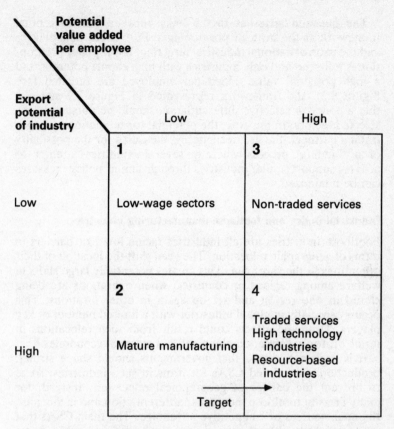

Figure 8.2 A framework for national industrial targeting in developed economies

obviously only be focused on one or a few firms. While the former can be stimulated through government support for domestic activities, such as R&D subsidies, the latter should only benefit from preset export-promoting measures such as export financing. This eliminates the possibility of shelter and subsequent microeconomic inefficiencies. Export promotion, however, certainly does not imply conventional export subsidies, which may lead to countervail actions under GATT procedures. (They also involve the subsidization of foreign consumption.) Finally, policies aimed at developing human capital are the cornerstone of any effective industrial targeting policy. If insufficient human capital is available to perform highly skilled jobs, the industrial policy collapses in spite of measures aimed at stimulating increased R&D activity.

The question arises as to the links between our conceptual framework on the strategic positioning of FSA-developing policies and the issue of national industrial targeting. If our policy prescription is followed and only industries with high export potential and a high potential value added per employee are targeted (see Figure 8.2), the framework represented in Figure 8.1 suggests that a policy of selective differentiation should be pursued in the selected sectors. In this way, the potential for retaliation by larger trading partners, the use of sheltering measures, or the possibility of a 'bidding' process whereby several countries attempt to actively support similar industries through similar policy measures can be minimized.

Industrial policy and footloose manufacturing industries

Footloose industries are all industries facing low exit barriers in terms of geographic relocation. They can shift the location of their operations in the short run. This creates potentially large shifts in welfare among regions or countries, when operations are being closed in one region and set up again in other locations. This occurs especially in global industries with a limited number of key players. Dramatic effects could result from such relocations in terms of, for example, employment and external economies.[11]

It is useless to argue that governments should shape strong, production cost-related CSAs for firms in such industries, so as to prevent the danger of geographical relocation. Instead, for many firms in footloose industries, differentiation and niching are the main sources of competitive advantage. The main CSAs that government should enhance are the availability of public infrastructure and human capital.

Another incorrect implication of the existence of footloose industries would be to limit the degree of foreign ownership in industry, building upon the belief that domestic ownership would make exit more difficult. While exit barriers may indeed be higher in the short run for domestically owned companies, it should be emphasized that their 'needs' in terms of strong CSAs are the same as those of foreign-owned companies. Higher geographical exit barriers in the short run hardly contribute to national wealth, when this weakens the domestic firms' competitive positions in world markets. On the contrary, an optimal industrial policy consists of creating a business environment attractive to foreign firms. If CSAs are sufficiently strong to encourage FDI by foreign firms in the economy, this is an indicator of public policy effectiveness, rather than a source of public policy concern. Moreover, as globalization increases, especially in industries where marketing and service aspects of niching require each firm to be close to its customers, foreign ownership should increase, not only in small open economies, but also in large markets. In global firms, decisions on location are not made as a function of the nationality of top managers or large equity holders. They result from a more objective analysis of the costs and benefits characteristic of different locations. In the long run, domestic firms, if they wish to remain competitive, will be guided by similar location considerations as foreign-owned firms.

If the use of trade barriers (protection) is excluded, as is mostly the case with a small open economy, footloose industries can still be tied down by increasing exit barriers. A conventional method of doing this, through government policy, is to subsidize large investments which are location-specific in technologically driven industries. However, such policies can only be successful in the long run if complemented by high exit barriers in terms of availability of human capital and excellent public infrastructure. In the long run, the main sunk cost prohibiting exit then becomes people-embodied and not machine-embodied.

Conclusion

In this chapter we discussed the rationale for an active industrial policy in a small open economy. One of the main assumptions in this chapter is that, in most countries, politicians and bureaucrats are in favour of some form of industrial policy. Hence, if the level of government intervention is fixed, the question arises as to how efficient industrial policy measures should be formulated and implemented. We demonstrated that four different types of FSA-developing policies can be pursued: rational imitation, defensive reaction, selective differentiation and total differentiation. We argued that selective differentiation is the optimal option for a small open economy faced with larger trading partners. Here, free trade is being pursued, combined with 'niched' industrial policy measures. Specific industrial policy issues were discussed, such as the entry barriers faced by small firms when penetrating larger foreign markets, and the stimulation of innovation. As to the former, we suggested the development of generally available programmes aimed at eliminating natural market imperfections. With respect to the stimulation of innovation, we argued in favour of measures aimed at creating substantial spillover effects in the national economy: free trade in high-technology goods should be combined with support for domestic R&D activities. The controversial issue of industrial targeting was also dealt with. Here we suggested that industrial niching policies should only be pursued in sectors with a high export potential and a high potential value added per employee.

Finally, we discussed the problem of creating exit barriers for footloose industries. We suggested policy measures aimed at raising the availability of human capital and developing an excellent public infrastructure, both for domestically-owned and foreign-owned firms.

Chapter nine

Industrial policy and global competition: Ontario's experience

The creation of efficient industrial policies

This chapter investigates the links between industrial policy and the international trade and investment strategies of firms faced with global competition. The problems faced by businesses competing in a global environment characterized by the power of the 'triad' economies of Japan, North America and the European Community have been analysed by the authors in the previous chapters.[1] It is useful to relate this analysis to the framework developed in this book.

First, in Chapter 3 it was argued that government should primarily pursue an efficiency-based trade policy. The main danger associated with the pursuit of distributional objectives is that trade policy may become an instrument of business firms engaged in non-efficiency strategies and seeking shelter. In addition, the importance of a suitable organizational structure to conduct trade policy was already emphasized, as it was shown how national trade policy objectives could be subverted in the policy implementation stage, in the case of a structure sensitive to the needs of pressure groups.

Second, Chapter 6 extended the framework developed in Chapter 3. The main policy conclusion is that interventionist trade policy measures can also be efficient in the long run in global industries if they are FSA-developing. An FSA-developing policy implies that trade policy measures aim at improving the international competitive position of the firms benefiting from these government measures. We argued that the success of an FSA-developing policy heavily depends upon the selection of firms and industries getting government support. Moreover, effective structural arrangements must be designed which are suitable for the implementation of government trade policy (for example independent agencies not dominated by pressure groups, use of

119

performance requirements, self-liquidating nature of government intervention, and insulation of programmes from changes in political leadership).

Third, in Chapter 7 the idea was developed that, from an efficiency perspective, the presence of some foreign ownership in the economy should not be viewed as the result of a failing trade-related industrial policy. The presence of foreign MNEs with strong FSAs should be welcomed, especially in small open economies which have a strong home base of MNEs themselves. Hence, discriminatory measures against foreign involvement in the economy should be avoided.

Fourth, Chapter 8 developed a strategic model of industrial policy. The main conclusion is that small open economies should follow a policy of selective differentiation; this implies that a cooperative attitude should be developed towards large trading partners, aiming at the achievement of freer trade without, however, jeopardizing national sovereignty as defined in Chapter 7. In addition, an active industrial policy should build upon the administrative heritage of the country involved and should attempt to be different from policies conducted abroad; governments too should seek 'niches' when developing industrial policy measures.

Fifth, Chapter 8 described in more detail the possible content of an efficient industrial policy in a small, developed open economy. Support should only be granted to industries characterized by both a high potential value added per employee and a high export potential. Government should not attempt to seek winners itself; programmes should be generally available to firms that fulfil pre-set criteria. Two problems may obviously arise here. The first problem is related to the limited number of viable companies in global industries (such as the civil aircraft industry). In such a case government may be forced to pick a potential future winner in a particular industry. The second problem is that the government agency responsible for picking winners must be able to pursue efficiency-based national trade policy objectives, related to the achievement of dynamic internal and external economies. Only if the government agency involved has the capacity to function independently from pressure exerted by firms seeking shelter and politicized decisions are avoided can bureaucratic discretion lead to efficiency.

However, the administrative heritage of industrial policy decision making in a particular region or country may suggest that the second problem described above cannot be solved effectively, within the framework of existing institutions. In such a case, bureaucratic discretion in the implementation of industrial policy measures should be avoided or a completely new agency must be set up with strong competences and a high autonomy to serve particular industrial policy goals.

Is bureaucratic and political discretion required to allow 'conditionality' when introducing industrial policy measures? If business firms agree to fulfil specific requirements, for example in terms of innovation or reinvestment or as quid pro quo for government support, government must have the ability to monitor the performance of the firms involved and to enforce the conditions upon which they agreed. In reality, the introduction of such conditions may adversely affect the performance of firms in high-technology industries if they limit the strategic flexibility of business firms to allocate resources in response to market conditions. In addition they may be ineffective in declining industries if they force firms to reinvest earnings in activities already characterized by excess capacity and low profits. In other words, if an administrative heritage of in-depth knowledge of industry and market conditions by government agencies is lacking, the introduction of *ex post* conditionality elements in industrial policy should be avoided. In such a case government should limit itself to the use of *ex ante* conditions by carefully defining the criteria to be fulfilled in order to become eligible for government support.

Here this theoretical framework is applied to explain a new global trading phenomenon: the recent escalation of industrial policies in many nations, where the focus is often upon the promotion of 'high-tech' sectors. Such policies are actually a form of subsidy which can adversely affect the environment for corporations when used as a strategic weapon by protected firms against their trading rivals. As an example of public policy in this area the recent report of the Premier's Council of Ontario is examined in detail.

Rugman and McIlveen found that most of the successful Canadian multinational enterprises are in resource-based industries, with only Northern Telecom and Moore Business Forms being active in the 'high-tech' areas which are normally thought of as the domains of the world's largest multinationals.[2] Yet the managers of these resource-based multinationals have exhibited considerable strategic management skills in positioning their product lines in world markets. They have organized the harvesting, processing and distribution of resource-based product lines in a scientific manner. Today, the FSAs of the resource-based Canadian multinationals are just as strong, if not stronger, than the proprietary knowledge advantage of the more traditional high-tech multinationals from foreign nations.

121

The key reasons for the success of the largest Canadian multinationals are related more to private sector management of a value-added chain than to government help from subsidies for technology in the form of an industrial strategy for Canada. However, the relatively low level of R&D expenditures in Canadian firms, as well as the relative lack of internationally competitive high-technology firms in many industries has often been considered a major weakness of the Canadian economy. This results in it being a source of public policy concern. We need to be concerned about the optimal design of an industrial policy for a small open economy such as Canada. In this paper, a conceptual framework will be developed – building upon the previous chapters – to help us assess the relative effectiveness of various industrial policy measures.

Industrial policy and global competition

The report of the Premier's Council of Ontario, published in mid-1988, states that active policies are required to create and sustain Canadian multinational enterprises.[3] These MNEs need strong FSAs in order to overcome entry barriers in larger markets. The report recognizes the existence of strong resource-based multinationals in Ontario and Canada, but finds a relative lack of such firms in high-growth, non-resource-based sectors.

Three major related problems are identified in the report:

1 the low level of R&D across industries;
2 the lack of niching strategies based upon innovative product differentiation;
3 insufficient government support for firms competing internationally and on the threshold of becoming true multinationals.

To overcome these problems the report recommends that government intervene selectively in favour of stimulating growth and higher value added in indigenous traded businesses (those exposed to strong international competition) which will remain, or become, internationally competitive in terms of exports.

The seven objectives identified by the Premier's Council as guiding its strategy are broad enough to be acceptable to virtually all private-sector and government groups. The objectives are to:

1 encourage 'competitive higher value added per employee' in all industries;

2   'focus industrial assistance' on traded sectors;
3   emphasize the growth of 'major indigenous Ontario companies of world scale' in the traded sectors;
4   'create an entrepreneurial, risk taking culture';
5   'build a strong science and technology infrastructure';
6   'improve the education, training and labor adjustment infrastructure';
7   follow a 'consensus approach' in creating economic strategies and programmes.

The key objective: indigenous multinationals

Of these the key objective would appear to be the third; it calls for the development of large indigenous multinational enterprises. Earlier, in summarizing the economic challenge facing Canada the Premier's Council lays the foundation for this conclusion when it states:

> Success in the high-growth industries of today and the emerging industries of tomorrow will require a set of economic skills we have not yet mastered. Primarily these are the talents required for creating and sustaining multinational enterprises which compete, not on the basis of low labor or raw materials costs, but rather through a process of continual renewal of their products, their systems, their factories, and their people.

Later the Council is even more explicit in its recognition of the need for support structures for indigenous multinationals:

> As the Council has examined the adequacy of our current economic situation, a number of structural and competitive weaknesses have come to light. Chief among these is the lack of a healthy base of indigenous Ontario multinational companies in non-resource industries.

The Council also identifies low R&D spending, too many 'undifferentiated commodity-type products', small-scale plants in core industries and an inadequate support climate (of both technology and human capital) for both small and large business. In particular, the Council states:

> The lack of support for threshold firms is of particular concern because it will be from the ranks of such companies that the indigenous multinationals of the future can emerge.

123

Free trade and global strategy

This consistent theme concerning the need to develop multi-national enterprises is undoubtedly correct in today's interdependent global economic system. Today multinationals from the triad powers of Japan, the EC and the United States dominate world trade and investment.[4] However, the Premier's Council exhibits amazing myopia by refusing to link the trend towards globalization to the need for access to one of the triad markets, in Canada's case, to the United States through the Free Trade Agreement. The Council's only reference to free trade is in the following elliptical statement:

> The adjustments taking place in the core industries in Ontario are driven by maturing markets and intensifying international competition. While the proposed Canada–US Free Trade Agreement may accelerate the adjustment process, it will not change it fundamentally.

But what if the Free Trade Agreement had *not* been passed? Surely failure to gain increased access to the US market would not have helped Canada, or Ontario, achieve the development of large-scale indigenous multinationals? In fact, the Premier's Council has been fortunate; now that the Free Trade Agreement is in force there are opportunities to achieve its objectives. Without free trade they were obviously unrealistic, as Rugman (1988c) has shown.

An assessment of the Premier's Council Report

The report states that mature manufacturing and resource-based industries have been the core of wealth creation in Canada. It argues, however, that today both types of businesses are generally characterized by relatively slow growth and increased international competition. Therefore, the report calls for a government focus on the expansion of high-growth sectors. In addition, it is argued that mature manufacturing in Canada lacks 'indigenous world-scale companies'. These are necessary for (1) strategic management decisions on resource allocation from a Canadian base; (2) R&D and marketing activities from a Canadian base; and (3) the development of 'infrastructure' activities, including finance and R&D decisions from a Canadian base. As a result, dynamic external economies in Canada are rather low. This simplistic belief in the value of high-technology firms over resource-based firms has been criticized in the past, for example by Rugman (1985).

A somewhat more balanced view of the role of resource-based firms appears in a recent report by the Canadian Institute for Advanced Research (1988).

Although it is recognized that non-indigenous firms should also be stimulated to expand, emphasis is placed on trying to become more like Sweden through support for indigenous firms. The Premier's Council viewpoint on Sweden appears to neglect the two-way nature of foreign direct investment, including foreign-based multinationals within Sweden.[5] Similarly, the role of non-indigenous subsidiaries in Canada, which benefit from their parents' FSAs, is still substantial. The inefficient tariff factories and purely branch plants of the past, which lacked autonomy, are no longer representative of foreign-based subsidiaries in Canada.[6] It should also be recognized that Ontario already has a large number of core resource-based and mature manufacturing multinationals characterized by strong FSAs. In its discussion of government policy, the Premier's Council report emphasizes the failure of past government support programmes for industry, both national and provincial ones. They usually fail for reasons of (1) pursuing distributional objectives; (2) insufficient selectivity (for example towards traded and high-growth businesses); and (3) unadapted support tools, such as promoting fixed asset investments instead of intangible infrastructure efforts (R&D, marketing know-how, etc.), which are very important in most high-growth industries.

The Premier's Council considers that only a limited number of existing programmes are effective. These include the Export Development Corporation and the Federal Defence Industry Productivity programmes, which focus both on high growth and traded industries. In terms of training, the Premier's Council has a sensible emphasis upon training for competitiveness.

The successful industries in Ontario identified at various stages by the Council are aerospace, telecommunications equipment, autos, steel and basic chemicals. Those with work to do to become internationally competitive include food processing, forest products, speciality chemicals, rubber, computers and biotechnology. This is a reasonable breakdown and one of the strengths of the Premier's Council report is Volume II, with its descriptive and analytical work on industry performance, competitiveness, market shares and strategic positioning. The use of modern analytical concepts from business policy is welcome.

Unfortunately, the prescriptive part of the Premier's Council Report (Volume I), mainly based upon a study of industrial policies in other countries such as Sweden, France, West Germany

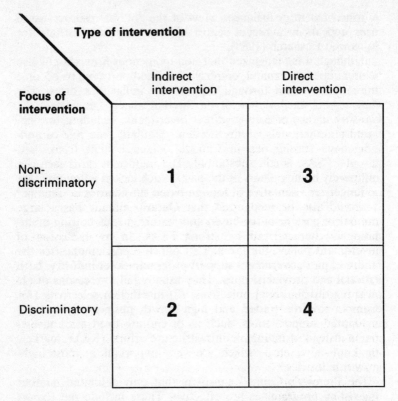

Figure 9.1 The nature of industrial policy

and Japan, published in Volume III, appears to bear little relationship to the analytical work of Volume II. The first volume demonstrates an erroneous view of the potential effectiveness of industrial policy in a small open economy faced with an environment characterized by triad power. This can be clarified through the use of Figure 9.1 on the nature of industrial policy.

A model of the nature of industrial policy

The horizontal axis of Figure 9.1 captures the types of government intervention, either indirect or direct. Indirect intervention refers here to the promotion of the infrastructure and such environmental factors as support for human capital, as well as the development of generally available measures in favour of business firms and industries. It is of primary importance that these firms and industries meet preset criteria, with minimal bureaucratic discretion or politicized choices occurring in the implementation stage. In contrast, direct intervention means discretionary choice by bureaucrats and politicians in the implementation stage. Thus, with direct intervention there is a lack of general availability of the programme for all firms that meet preset conditions. This may then lead to the creation of shelter for the programme beneficiaries if the implementors are sensitive to the demands of pressure groups and are not equipped to pursue efficiency-based objectives. The administrative heritage of industrial policy in Ontario, also described in Volume 1 of the report, precisely indicates a lack of efficiency in the implementation of industrial policy programmes.

The vertical axis distinguishes between the focus of intervention, either discriminatory or non-discriminatory. Discriminatory measures here relate to government intervention in favour of firms with domestic ownership or domestically located corporate headquarters (i.e. indigenous firms). It also refers to government intervention in favour of firms located in the province of Ontario. In contrast, non-discriminatory measures do not favour indigenous over non-indigenous firms; nor do they favour Ontario firms over firms from other provinces.

Figure 9.1 represents four types of industrial policy that can be pursued by a national or provincial government. It is our view that only an industrial policy positioned in quadrant 1 can be effective for a small open economy such as Canada faced with external protectionist trading partners and an administrative heritage of shelter-based industrial policy.

Effectiveness refers here to the actual contribution of government support to the development of multinational activity in Canada, taking into account negative secondary effects of this support on the national economy. Non-discriminatory measures are thus more effective than discriminatory ones in favour of indigenous firms. The latter type of support neglects the important role of domestic subsidiaries of foreign-based multinationals in Canada.[7] In addition, discrimination in favour of companies located in a particular sub-national territory (such as a province) should be avoided. This leads to the generation of competitive bidding amongst provincial governments, which results in welfare losses at the national level.[8]

Direct intervention in the form of support for particular firms or industries as a result of bureaucratic discretion or politicized choices in the implementation stage should be avoided, for different reasons, even if used in a non-discriminatory fashion. First, direct intervention may initiate sheltering strategies of business

127

firms. This occurs if the institutional structure through which industrial policy is implemented is characterized by a high sensitivity to clientele groups.[9] Second, such support, if characterized by high visibility, may lead to protectionist reactions of larger trading partners. This occurs in the form of countervail and anti-dumping actions, or attempts to negotiate voluntary export restraints.

Direct intervention may also stimulate foreign governments to protect their domestic companies based on the infant industry argument, the old industry argument, or the dynamic internal and external economic arguments associated with the theory of strategic trade policy.[10] In all of these cases, the asymmetry in size and international economic significance of industrial policy measures of the small open economy and its larger trading partner should stimulate the former to refrain from direct intervention. In other words, only a policy located in quadrant 1 is consistent with the policy prescription of selective differentiation developed in Chapter 8.

The fourteen recommendations reviewed

The conceptual framework developed above will now be applied to the recommendations formulated by the Premier's Council of Ontario. In each case, the recommendations will be positioned in one of the quadrants of Figure 9.1, and will be assessed using the policy prescriptions set out in the previous section.

To deal with the problems of lack of international competitiveness in Ontario the Council makes fourteen recommendations. These recommendations are broken down into six categories, consistent with the groupings in the Council's report. Here only the most important recommendations will be discussed in detail. These are themes not only relevant to Ontario, but also to Canada as a whole.

Core industries

1   The creation of an Ontario Recapitalization Incentive Plan (ORIP). This would give tax incentives to investors engaging in equity investments in middle-sized (minimum 50 employees in Ontario), high-growth, export-oriented 'indigenous' businesses.

This is potentially an effective measure, but only if it is implemented in a non-discriminatory, indirect manner. This means the support must be made available to both indigenous and non-indigenous firms, and there must be no bureaucratic involvement which could lead to unintended policy outputs. It is export promoting if it builds upon the FSAs of companies. It also helps to compensate for possible capital market imperfections faced by smaller firms when confronted with entry barriers in foreign markets. However, ORIP, as described in the report, is discriminatory in nature, as it is targeted towards indigenous firms only. This places it in quadrant 2 of Figure 9.1. Thus, it must be altered so that it will fit into quadrant 1.

2 The creation of a 'sound industrial restructuring process' for exporting firms that have become unprofitable, but with viable 'restructuring opportunities'.

This measure should be rejected on the basis that it represents direct intervention of a discriminatory nature, placing it in quadrant 4. This will probably lead to corporate 'shelter', by allocating money in response to corporate pressure groups. This is especially likely to occur since it is proposed that labour should be involved in restructuring decisions. In their formulation of this proposal the Council argues that firms with no prospect of long-term survival or without a viable restructuring plan will not be supported. Yet how this will be implemented in practice is obscure.

Recommendation number 3 deals with worker adjustment, which is necessary in times of major structural change, of which the Free Trade Agreement is a perfect example. It is an acceptable recommendation, in quadrant 1, as it is an indirect, non-discriminatory measure. However, it is only acceptable if it is a temporary programme. If it has no sunset clause, it would tend to drift towards quadrant 2.

Recommendation number 4 suggests worker ownership programmes be implemented. This recommendation cannot be evaluated precisely in terms of discrimination or directness, given that the Council does not elaborate on the exact role government will play. If anything, it is probably in quadrant 2. Interestingly, no supporting reasoning is given as to why such a programme is necessary for core industries to succeed. Rather than being a useful policy, it is more a result of the 'consensus' mentality of the Council.

High-Growth and Emerging Industries

5 Tax incentives will be given to firms which engage in incremental R&D expenditures above their previous three year rolling average of R&D performed in Ontario.

This measure is also directly interventionist and discriminatory in nature, placing it in quadrant 4. Can this measure be restricted to only a few, selected industries that have high growth potential? Will such tax incentives not lead, eventually, to competitive bidding among provinces? The implementation of such measures should be undertaken by the federal government, not by provincial authorities. Further, this could be considered an export subsidy by companies in the United States, leading to possible countervail actions which would negate the effectiveness of such incentives.

6 A 'strategic approach' by the Ontario government, including Ontario Hydro, to procurement will be introduced to (a) develop Canadian firms, especially in the medical and pharmaceutical industries, and stimulate foreign MNEs to engage in R&D in the province; and (b) award small contracts to Ontario firms, which would allow them to build up the necessary capacity in technological know-how (e.g., design of prototypes) prior to the existence of a contract to bid on. As a result they may eventually be granted large contracts as the base upon which a strong company can be built.

This measure should be rejected, as it is directly interventionist and discriminatory (quadrant 4). It will lead to competition among the provinces at the expense of Canadian welfare. Long-run strategic procurement should not be implemented if other bidders already have the required technology. Which person or persons in the provincial bureaucracy or elsewhere would have the ability to pick out the 'winners' who may some day develop a technology which proves to be a strong FSA? This policy would probably lead to continuous shelter for companies identified as the province's 'chosen instruments'. In addition, the Strategic Procurement Committee developed to match government needs with suitable firms is another level of bureaucracy, creating an impediment for suitable bidders on government contracts whose firms may be arbitrarily deemed not to be 'strategic'. Finally, international competition would not be fostered by making firms dependent on government contracts for their survival; on the contrary, the development of sheltering behaviour will be stimulated.

Risk sharing with threshold firms

7 A risk-sharing fund will provide incentives to successful exporting firms when engaging in new product development, prototype placement abroad and the creation of new marketing

offices outside North America (up to 50 per cent of the project). Repayment depends on the success of the project: no payment if the project fails; above market rate if it succeeds.

This measure again is to be rejected on the basis of its directly interventionist, discriminatory nature (quadrant 4). If a company is truly successful and not in its infant stage anymore, why would it need government to intervene directly, providing support in the form of capital? If a project is sound and a firm already established, funds will mostly be provided by the capital market, especially since many threshold companies are former subsidiaries or divisions or spin-offs of MNEs. It is then argued that this support would be primarily aimed at forty to fifty non-resource-based firms in Ontario, which are on the 'threshold' of becoming MNEs (sales between 40 million and 400 million Canadian dollars) but which may be 'betting the company' on single new projects. Even if they are not 'betting the company', it is argued that they may be confronted with serious problems such as:

(a) the move from a 'cloner' to an innovator, requiring high innovation expenditures;
(b) 'simultaneous market' penetration which requires them to market new products on different markets simultaneously to beat global competition;
(c) the 'stuck in a niche' problem whereby growth requires a firm to go beyond its niche and enter new market segments often at high risks.

In any case, the choice of which firms are deserving of such support will be a discriminatory process involving substantial bureaucratic or political discretion in the implementation stage. Given the administrative heritage of Ontario's past industrial policies, the probability of this measure leading to wealth-creating effects seems limited, although this type of measure could in principle be efficient when entry barriers to foreign market penetration with new products are high (see pp. 111–13).

8 The Ontario Development Corporations (ODCs) should be restructured. Until now they have not been selective in giving support and have in fact provided shelter to small businesses and industries facing difficulties. They should provide funds for R&D and marketing to high growth industries, especially middle-sized firms keen to export.

This is a direct, discriminatory, quadrant 4 measure; the ODCs already exist but they provide shelter. If their policies can be shifted towards FSA development, this should be encouraged. However, their poor track record raises the question: would it not be more useful to eliminate them altogether, especially since it is proposed that the ODCs would remain responsible for assisting in regional development (i.e. pursuing distributional objectives)? How would they be able to distinguish between equity-based support serving local needs and support to turn small firms into major exporters? Again, the influence of corporate lobbyists and public pressures cannot be ignored when evaluating the ability of a political organization to choose FSA-developing rather than sheltering situations as being worthy of support.

Improving the entrepreneurial climate for traded businesses

9   Tax exemptions will be given to venture capitalists investing in manufacturing or traded services, to the extent that these businesses (up to a minimum of $10 million in sales in a first stage) have a commitment to engage in substantial exports within five years, and will direct operations from an Ontario base.

While this can be implemented through indirect government involvement, it is still discriminatory, placing it in quadrant 2. This proposal could be effective in theory for the same reasons as the former proposal, i.e. if FSA-developing activities are viable. However, the assumption is again being made that the financial market will not support a viable firm with an enticing export opportunity. Further, the exemptions are contingent on certain commitments being made, such as the firm being 'committed to achieving substantial export sales over the next five years'. Commitments such as these are easily broken, leading to manipulative activities on the part of beneficiaries of the government programme.[11]

10   Tax incentives will be given to investors in initial public stock offerings of Ontario corporations. These incentives will be more important than the ones provided by the Ontario Recapitalization Incentive Plan (ORIP). The main advantage will be to enhance the liquidity of venture capital investments.

This measure has the merit of being more indirect than most of the others, and aims at decreasing financial market imperfections by improving the liquidity of venture capital investments. However, the difficulty is implementing it in a non-discriminatory manner. If that is possible, then the measure is a useful recommendation, as it could be moved from quadrant 2 to quadrant 1.

Meeting the science and technology imperative

11 Government funded R&D should be redirected towards business priorities.

It is useful (1) to enhance clearly targeted R&D efforts in universities and government laboratories and (2) to promote cooperation with the private sector, (for example through 'Ontario Centers of Excellence' which will advance basic research and supply advanced technical personnel in the industry). The government should not reallocate substantial R&D resources (20 per cent of current in-house research) to industry. How would priorities be set to allocate such 'gifts' to the private sector? Again the problem of direct, discriminatory intervention leading to shelter arises (quadrant 4).

There is an important implicit contradiction in this proposal. On the one hand it is stated that R&D efforts as a percentage of GDP in Canada are much lower than in other advanced nations. The primary reason for this is alleged insufficient R&D in industry, for which government has attempted to compensate by in-house R&D. These attempts were not successful because selectivity towards particular business needs was lacking. In view of this failure, it is argued that government should now redirect its efforts towards these industry needs. However, if the private sector is not satisfying its alleged needs itself, how can it be expected that government, which already has a very poor track record in this area, could now suddenly solve this problem for the industry?

The problem is that:

(a) Low R&D results primarily from an industry focus in Canadian firms on marketing, for example, in resource-based industries. In this context it should be emphasized that the level of government performed R&D expressed as a percentage of GNP equals 0.32 in Canada as compared to 0.13 in Sweden, 0.28 in Japan and 0.33 in Germany (data for 1983) (when including research in universities these figures are respectively 0.64; 0.53; 0.85; 0.73).[12] These percentages indicate that successful advanced economies do not necessarily need high government spending on R&D.

(b) Although R&D is low in foreign subsidiaries of MNEs, this hardly reflects low international competitiveness as these

133

companies benefit from strong FSAs of parent companies, which may have centralized R&D facilities in their home country for micro-efficiency reasons.

(c) Increased global competition and innovation even in mature and resource-based industries (and resulting entry barriers) may indeed require an increase of R&D in Canadian firms. But this is better stimulated by substantial selective tax incentives or R&D investments (by the implementation of recommendations 1, 3, 9 and 10).

12 A technical personnel assistance programme will be created which will give a subsidy of 50 per cent of new employees salaries in the first year and 25 per cent in the second year to exporting firms (with less than $100 million in sales) that hire technicians, engineers and scientists.

This proposal should also be rejected, as it falls into quadrant 4. In addition to being directly interventionist, this recommendation has the added shortcoming of not being able to separate firms that would not hire technical personnel without the subsidy from firms that would have hired the personnel in any case. Moreover, it seems hardly conceivable that a total subsidy of 75 per cent of a one-year wage would stimulate firms to hire technical or scientific personnel, especially since going concern motives are predominant when hiring such personnel. In other words, a comparatively more efficient system would be the introduction of low (or zero) interest loans, for example, for 5 years, which would cover part of the expenses of new technical or scientific personnel.

In addition, Canadian firms should attempt to develop strategic alliances in order to build technology-based FSAs; however, this would seem to be more a problem of corporate strategy than a public policy concern. Such alliances should focus especially on precompetitive research and the commercialization of new technology (including export promotion). In Canada, both federal and provincial governments could stimulate the formation of such alliances through a system of advisory committees involving both senior public officials and the top managers of business firms.

Investing in people

13 A 'comprehensive people strategy' will be elaborated in Ontario so as to improve the quality of supply of human capital for Ontario businesses.

This is a good proposal which could surely be implemented in an indirect, non-discriminatory manner. It could lead to comparatively higher efficiency to the extent that this implies a redirection of existing government scheduling on education and training towards programmes of more immediate use to business.

14 The final recommendation calls for the creation of Ontario Excellence Awards to recognize individuals for contributions to economic progress.

Will the members of the council be the first in line for these awards? And will the critics be last in line?

Conclusion

The Premier's Council of Ontario has produced a report with mixed qualities. The strengths of the report lie in the recognition of global competition and today's key instrument for doing international business – the multinational enterprise. It is a sensible policy prescription to develop the environmental infrastructure which supports the growth of Canadian-owned multinational enterprises and multinational activity in general. Thus, the identification of labour training and adjustment policies, educational programmes and general fiscal investment incentives (if kept non-discriminatory) is to be welcomed.

The problems in the Premier's Council report relate to recommendations which move beyond the development of the infrastructure and business environment, or even the support of selected firms and industries through preset criteria, towards schemes that include extensive bureaucratic discretion in the implementation stage and are of a strongly discriminatory nature. The effective implementation of such measures will require insight into the nature of the competitive process, which has so far eluded even the best-prepared government officials and politicians in Canada. Recommendations which include important bureaucratic and political involvement in the implementation of such programmes as R&D grants, strategic government procurement and discriminatory investment incentives are unlikely to be successful in terms of developing multinational activity in Canada. Unfortunately, the great majority of the Premier's Council recommendations (at least seven) are in quadrant 4 of Figure 9.1, being directly interventionist and discriminatory; another four are in quadrant 2, while at present only three may fit in the desirable first quadrant.

Governments, including ones as large and powerful as that of the Province of Ontario, should continue to improve the nature of business and government relations. Policies which improve the climate for business enterprise and contribute to the elimination of natural and government imposed market imperfections are required. There is no need for government to do the job of business through a direct and discriminatory industrial and trade policy in Ontario.

Chapter ten

Conclusion

The global economy and efficient management

We have recognized in this book that today international business is characterized by the emergence of three large trading blocs in the world. The triad powers of the United States, Japan, and the European Community now dominate world trade and investments. These triad nations are the homes of giant multinational enterprises. Over half of all the world's traded output is conducted by five hundred large multinational enterprises, virtually all of them located in the triad powers. Managers and policy makers are interacting in a process which, we believe, is leading to greater degrees of protectionism, adding layers of complexity to corporate strategy.

The trend towards the globalization of industry and the emergence of large multinational enterprises based on the triad has changed the thinking of managers and policy makers. In Europe, the drive for a single internal market by 1992 is creating a minor revolution in the strategic planning of corporations doing business there. In Canada, to help secure access to the market of the United States, the private sector supported the negotiation and implementation of the Canada–US Free Trade Agreement over the 1986–8 period. This was primarily a response to the perceived use of 'administered protection' by US companies. Now strategic planners are busy gearing up for operations in an integrated North American market. Managers in all corporations are now preparing for business in the global economy.

Large business units are already being developed, especially in Canada (and similar-sized nations), in order to survive the intense competition from large multinationals in the United States, Europe and Japan. Strategies are being developed for corporations to compete on price, by differentiation, or by finding niches in both goods and service markets. The recent wave of mergers

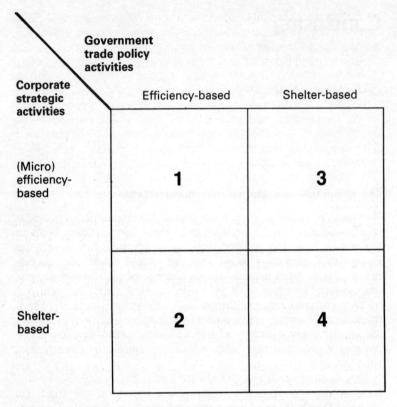

Figure 10.1 Efficiency- and shelter-based activities of firms and governments

and acquisitions is an inevitable result of globalization and trade liberalization. It is an efficient process by which managers and economies prepare to survive into the twenty-first century.

This book has attempted to analyse business–government inter-actions in the realm of trade policy from a strategic management perspective. The core conclusions resulting from our analysis can be described through the use of Figure 10.1.

Efficiency versus shelter

The normative point of view taken in this study is that the present tendency towards globalization requires both firms and govern-ments to develop efficiency-based activities (quadrant 1). Micro-economic efficiency is required in the long run to compete with global rivals, especially in host countries. The dangers associated with a shelter-based strategy were clearly spelt out in earlier sections. Government in turn should pursue national efficiency-based policies. In the long run, shelter imposes welfare losses on society.

From a theoretical point of view it could be argued that contradictions may exist between the pursuit of micro-economic efficiency at the firm level and national efficiency at the country level. In practice, and especially in a dynamic perspective, the inefficiencies of particular trade policy measures are similar. If long-run shelter is introduced through protectionist trade policy measures, managers and workers will not be as motivated to maximize the firm's output/input ratio as compared to a situation without shelter. Thus too many inputs will be used for given outputs.

The main contribution of our work has been to demonstrate the interaction between business and government policies. Business firms engaged in shelter-based strategies may subvert the realization of national efficiency-based trade policies, thus pushing government agencies to develop activities on the right-hand side of Figure 10.1. Similarly, if trade policy regulations and government agencies responsible for trade policy formation are biased in favour of comparatively inefficient domestic companies this may stimulate domestic firms to shift from the upper side of Figure 10.1 to the lower side. In our view it is the combination of the two elements mentioned above which is now pushing the United States towards the fourth quadrant.

Nevertheless, the Canada–US Free Trade Agreement now exists to offset this tendency. We feel that the signing of this agreement, which will bring high economic benefits to both nations, is largely due to the active involvement of business firms with strong FSAs located on both sides of the border. They have been able to create a shift in both US and Canadian government trade policy towards the first quadrant.

We are convinced that the ability of business firms, especially multinationals, to bring about this shift of government policy from the third to the first quadrant will be the true challenge for the 1990s. Global firms with strong FSAs are now probably the best guardians against the protectionist temptations both inside and outside the triad.

Sovereignty and corporate strategy

Nations like Canada are not economic islands. Instead, they are relatively small economic units in a sea of global competition.

Old-fashioned thinking about promoting sovereignty through protection and industrial policies is irrelevant in today's interdependent global economic system. In a relatively small open economy like Canada greater economic efficiency is conditional upon the promotion of FSAs within a climate of government support for infrastructure development.

Indeed, to enhance the efficiency of large companies in a country like Canada, more deregulation of the economy is necessary. For example, in Canada the beer industry is handicapped by historical interprovincial barriers to trade. The airline industry faces severe regulation, especially on domestic routes. The oil industry has been the victim of interventionist policies such as the National Energy Program. The development of energy and other sectors would be helped by a more stable climate for private-sector investment. All of these policies hinder the ability of Canadian companies to become better equipped to pursue successful competitive strategies against foreign rivals.

Today the world's multinational enterprises pursue three types of strategy. First, they compete on price, through global economies of scale and learning-curve effects. Second, they engage in product differentiation by advertising expenditures and making products into brand names. Third, they follow a focus strategy by seeking niches on geographical or product line bases. In all three areas the trend towards government protection and shelter hinders multinationals in their strategic planning. Instead, firms need to develop and exploit their own type of competitive strategy. There is sometimes the potential for cost savings through a larger scale of production. On other occasions there may be opportunities for the assembly of an optimal set of brand name products and their production on a world-wide basis. At times, niche strategies can be pursued by both large and small firms; they are most useful to larger firms when coupled with the development of scale or differentiation strategies. In contrast, shelter is never a viable long-term strategy.

Against this background of competitive global rivalry it has become apparent in this book why shelter is dangerous when doing business in the global economy. Neither companies protected by shelter, nor the nations abusing their legal and political systems to provide it, can develop sustainable competitive or comparative advantages. Indeed, it is extremely foolish for governments to continue to provide shelter as an alternative to efficiency-based strategic restructuring of business firms.

For small open economies, the days of xenophobia in both policy making and management are over; the future is in looking outward. Due to the emergence of new thinking by strategic planners, Canada and other relatively small open economies are now on the way to being competitive players in the global economy. Although the triad nations will probably continue to attempt to close their markets into regional trading blocs as an answer to demands of shelter-seeking firms, good managers will rely less on national strategies such as shelter and more on achieving international market entry by the development of cost-reducing and differentiation-enhancing capability. In this manner, the nature of global competition will discipline the recent surge of shelter-based strategies and lead to a more efficient global trading system.

Notes

Chapter 1 Introduction

1 See, for example, Porter (1986) and Rugman (1987).
2 See Rugman (1988d).
3 See Rugman and Anderson (1987).
4 See Winham (1987).
5 See Rugman and Anderson (1987a: ch. 6).
6 See Rugman and McIlveen (1985).

Chapter 2 Corporate strategic management

1 The major focus of this book will be on the trade-related aspects of the free-trade agreement, between Canada and the United States, especially the institutional context within which the US trade policy is currently implemented; investment issues have been discussed elsewhere (see Rugman 1987b, 1988e). There is a short discussion of investment policy in Chapter 7 of this book.
2 In practice it may be extremely difficult to distinguish between the creation of government intervention as a substitute for, or a complement of, a company's FSAs. Here the concept of strategic intent is crucial. Is the long-run objective of corporate management to use government intervention as the core element for the firm's success in the marketplace or is it merely a useful tool to enhance the firm's competitiveness in a regulated environment? For an analysis see Rugman and Verbeke (1988b).
3 Rugman develops such a model for multinational enterprises where FSAs are controlled by the firm and the CSAs are exogenously determined by principles of comparative advantage. See Rugman. (1981, 1986a and 1988b).
4 This is a form of 'unnatural' shelter, in the spirit of Rugman (1981).
5 We should emphasize that efficiency-based and non-efficiency-based strategies are not necessarily characterized by efficiency and inefficiency in the marketplace, in terms of output/input ratios. An efficiency-based strategy is a process of corporate behaviour; this can be pursued by a comparatively inefficient firm. In contrast, non-efficiency-based activities may, in principle, be developed by highly

efficient firms. In this context, it could even be argued that a firm may be 'efficient' in developing a non-efficiency-based strategy. A non-efficiency-based strategy refers to activities which do not aim at improving or realizing the firm's cost-reducing or differentiation-enhancing potential.

6 Well-known examples are the three generic strategies of Porter (1980, 1985), namely cost leadership, differentiation and focus, and the transaction cost theory of Oliver E. Williamson (1975, 1985).

7 Recent theories which analyse such strategies include the discussion of the behaviour of multinational enterprises towards sovereign host country governments, found in Doz (1986b).

8 See Leibenstein (1976).

9 Recently, Porter has recognized the existence of such protected market strategies in global industries (Porter 1986).

10 Strategic activities in the third and fourth quadrant may also complement each other. For example, in the case of voluntary export restraints, foreign exporters must cooperate among each other to allocate quotas. In addition, they may set high minimum prices so as not to upset less efficient domestic suppliers. Such restrictions on imports then facilitate collusion, tacitly or overtly, among domestic producers, so as to increase price–cost margins. An example is found in the US automobile industry where the heritage of industry collusion has led the firms involved to avoid the dissipation of the rents resulting from import restrictions on Japanese cars. See Kwoka (1984).

11 For a conceptual analysis of how Canadian business will react to trade liberalization between Canada and the United States, see Farrow and Rugman (1988) especially pp. 13–30. An overview of recent strategies adopted by Canadian multinationals can be found in Chapter 5.

12 For an overview of the empirical evidence, see Lipsey and Dobson (1987).

13 In this context, a successful adjustment programme has been defined as a 'temporary program that, within 5 or 10 years, ensures that the industry can once again meet international competition without further government intervention and that labour has been reemployed elsewhere in the economy' (Hufbauer and Rosen 1986: 2).

14 For an excellent overview of the evidence, see OECD (1985: ch. 5).

Chapter 3   Trade policy and corporate strategy

1 In terms of trade policy formation a distinction can be made between the political track in the United States (where the President and Congress are involved) and the technical track (where the US International Trade Commission and the Department of Commerce administer US trade laws in a supposedly non-political manner); see Finger *et al.* (1982).

2 Unfortunately, it is in practice difficult to realize this distinction, as

documented by Baldwin (1986). See also Lenway (1983) and Rugman and Anderson (1987a).

3 Many examples of self-serving behaviour by both politicians and bureaucrats may be found in, among others, Buchanan and Tullock (1962), Tullock (1965), Niskanen (1971), Breton (1974) and Mueller (1979).

4 Examples of such protectionist policies whereby pressure groups generate tariff barriers are given in Ethier (1983), Baldwin (1985) and Lenway (1983).

5 This is demonstrated in Lindblom (1977) and Olson (1965).

6 See Mayhew (1974). An application of this to trade policy can be found in Caves (1976).

7 See Lindsay (1976) and Brown and Jackson (1982).

8 It should be noted that although this discussion focuses on the recent extensive use of administered protection in America through the technical track, use of political track measures continues to occur. The prime example of this is the 'Super 301' bill passed in 1989, allowing American legislators to single out countries engaging in 'unfair trade practices', and impose retaliatory measures against them. Again, while Americans claim to be on the left-hand side of Figure 3.1 (efficiency based, cell 1 in this case), provisions such as the 'Super 301' can be a problem for American trading partners when the actual policy outcome (cell 3, non-efficiency based) is inconsistent with the stated intentions of the political track. For a further discussion, see Rugman and Anderson (1989).

9 Evidence that this has occurred is contained in Rugman and Anderson (1987a). They analysed fifty US countervail and anti-dumping cases against Canada in the 1980–6 period, including fish products, hogs and pork, other agricultural products, lumber, steel and many others.

10 See Rugman and Porteous (1988).

11 See Rugman and Anderson (1987a).

12 This is shown in Rugman and Anderson (1987a and b).

13 For an elaboration, see Rugman (1986b).

14 See Finger (1981).

15 For evidence and further explanation, see Destler (1986) and Finger *et al.* (1982).

16 See Rugman and Anderson (1987b).

17 ibid.

18 See Olson (1965). This view has been challenged by Milner (1987). She has argued that internationally oriented firms with strong FSAs and characterized by high exports, multinationality and global intra-firm trade have successfully influenced trade policy in the United States and France so as to limit protectionism. Although we agree with Milner's conclusions (see our own analysis in Chapter 4), it remains true that in some industries at least the needs of inefficient firms to obtain trade protection are much higher than the needs of efficient firms to resist this type of shelter.

19 This occurred partly since foreign policy goals have often determined its behaviour towards trade policy (see Bauer *et al.* 1972). It has been argued that the GATT reinforced the agencies of the executive branch in favour of free international trade (Lenway 1985).
20 See Finger and Nogues (1987).

Chapter 4 Corporate strategy for trade business

1 See Porter (1986) and Ohmae (1985).
2 See Rugman (1981) and Rugman *et al.* (1985).
3 See, for example, Olson (1965), Brock and Magee (1978). Baldwin uses public choice theory to provide a synthesis of studies that explain existing levels of protection in the United States on the basis of industry characteristics. See Baldwin (1985).
4 Developed by such authors as Lavergne (1981) and Ray (1981).
5 Several authors have argued that trade liberalization leads to increases in both direct investment and intra-firm trade by individual companies. See, for example, Safarian (1985) and Burgess (1985, 1986).
6 See Porter (1986).
7 See Rugman (1987a).
8 See Rugman (1988e).
9 See Rugman (1988a).
10 See Canada, DEA (1988).
11 See Hufbauer and Rosen (1986).
12 ibid.
13 See World Bank (1988) and Cline (1989).
14 See Hufbauer *et al.* (1986).
15 The efficiency advantages of the use of the escape clause as compared to legislative quotas and voluntary restraint arrangements are described in Lawrence (1989).
16 See Finger and Nogues (1987). Here, it was stated that 'over the period 1980–85 only 1 of 135 CVD cases initiated in Chile reached an affirmative final determination. In private conversation Chilean trade officials have informed us that a major consideration in Chile's decision to abandon the use of CVD's was the threat of retaliation by trading partners against whom cases were brought.'
17 ibid.
18 See Messerlin (1989).

Chapter 5 Global corporate strategy and the Free Trade Agreement

1 The model generated in this section of the paper weds the competitive strategy literature of Porter (1980, 1986) to the internalization theory of Rugman (1981) and Dunning and Rugman (1985). See also Rugman *et al.* (1985).
2 For a further discussion of the role of the Canadian MNE in the international marketplace and particularly with regard to the United States, see Rugman (1990).

3 For an overview of the empirical evidence, see Rugman and
   McIlveen (1985) and Rugman and Warner (1988). Their models
   show that it is possible to move up a value-added chain, building
   upon strong resource-based CSAs.
4 See Rugman and Verbeke (1988a).
5 See Baldwin and Gorecki (1986), Harris and Cox (1984) and Daly
   and MacCharles (1986).
6 See Wonnacott (1987). MacCharles (1987) has also emphasized this
   infra-firm adjustment. Lipsey and York (1988) report that this was
   the experience among MNEs in the formation of the European
   Economic Community.
7 Rugman (1988e).
8 See Rugman and Warner (1988).
9 See Rugman (1988a) and Rugman and Anderson (1987a).
10 See Rugman and McIlveen (1985).
11 See Rugman (1988c).
12 See Rugman and Porteous (1988).
13 See MacCharles (1987).
14 See Rugman (1987b).
15 See Canada, MSS (1988).
16 This simplistic view of these firms has been expressed by Baranson
   (1985).
17 See Crookell (1987).
18 See Newall (1988).
19 See Gove (1988).
20 See Coopers and Lybrand (1988) and Thorne and Thorne (1988).

Chapter 6 Trade and industrial policy in the Triad

1 In Canada, James Laxer (1987), the Premier's Council of Ontario
   (1988) and others have called for a similar type of industrial policy.
   The latter study is analysed in Chapter 9.
2 The CSAs capture the factor endowments of a nation, basically the
   variables in its aggregate production function (see Rugman 1981).
3 For example, see McCraw (1986) and work by some of his colleagues
   at the Harvard Business School.
4 See Rugman (1981).
5 It has been demonstrated that the US trade deficits merely result
   from the macro-economic imbalance between American spending
   and production, which itself is caused by the government deficit
   ranging between $150 billion and $200 billion. Moreover, the
   Japanese 'portion' of the US trade deficit has not increased
   substantially between 1981 and 1985, so that Japanese non-free
   trade strategies in favour of domestic firms cannot be held
   responsible for the rising import volume of the United States. See
   Lawrence and Litan (1987).
6 In the infant industry case, a fast-growing internal market and active
   competition between domestic firms are some of the requirements
   for achieving economic efficiency. See Brander (1987a). In the

profit-shifting case, subsidies and other advantages may be granted
by government to domestic firms to generate strategic effects (such
as deterring entry by potential foreign competitors) or dynamic scale
economies (learning curve effects). International competition is
required to stimulate cost efficiency and innovative behaviour of the
domestic firms. See Brander and Spencer (1985), Brander (1987a
and b).

7 Through countervailing actions, such as trade remedy laws, this
unfair competition can be restricted. See Hufbauer and Erb (1985).

8 See Leibenstein (1976).

9 See OECD (1985).

10 In this sense, Congress insulated itself from its own tendency to
subvert national free trade goals to which most members of
Congress agreed. See Destler (1986) and Finger *et al.* (1982).

11 See, for example, Yoffie (1986).

12 See Porter (1986).

13 See Ohmae (1987), and also Lawrence and Litan (1987).

14 See McCraw and O'Brien (1986).

15 See Doz (1986) and Tyson (1987).

16 See Yoffie (1986).

17 See Morici (1984).

18 See Ouchi (1984).

19 In generalizing about Japanese trade policy, Abegglen and Stalk
have emphasized that, in most cases, no national champions are
picked out by government, it is the marketplace that determines the
'winning' and 'losing' firms (see Abegglen and Stalk 1985).

20 Kapteijn and Van Themaat (1980).

21 Hosoya (1979).

22 For a thorough analysis see Pearce and Sutton (1986).

23 ibid.

24 See, for example, Norman (1986) and Curzon (1989).

25 See Cecchini (1988) and Commission of the European Communities
(1988).

Chapter 7   Globalization and national responsiveness

1 Perhaps the most influential of these studies is Cecchini (1988),
while Emerson *et al.* (1988) examine the economic benefits of 1992
in more detail. Both studies were commissioned by the EC. For a
more critical analysis, the study by the London Business School
(1989) is of interest, while an American viewpoint has been
produced for the National Planning Association by Michael
Calingaert (1988).

2 This is based on the work of Bartlett (1986).

3 ibid.

4 In fact, this move towards domestic and non-border consolidation
is already going on. Between 1 June 1987 and 31 May 1988, 225
domestic mergers occurred among the 1,000 largest EC firms (as
compared to 140 mergers in the comparable 1984–5 period). As to

the international mergers within the EC, there were more than 100 mergers in the same period between 1 June 1987 and 31 May 1988 (as compared with less than 50 mergers in 1984–5). Well-known examples include the acquisition of, for example, Buitoni and Rowntree by Nestlé and the acquisition of Grundig by Philips. See Friberg (1989).

5 Vandermerwe (1989).

6 It is a cell which is consistent with the 'staples' theory of economic development, popularized by Innis and other political economists at the University of Toronto. See Innis (1956). It is also a theory popularized in Grant (1965).

7 For further discussion of the effects of the Free Trade Agreement see Lipsey and York (1988).

8 See Rugman (1988f).

9 See Rugman (1987b).

10 See Rugman (1990).

11 These developments are discussed in detail in Rugman and McIlveen (1985).

12 Rugman (1987b).

13 ibid.

14 This is discussed in Rugman (1988d).

Chapter 8 An industrial policy for a small open economy

1 Caves (1982).

2 A major advantage derived from free trade for firms located in a small open economy may then be company rationalization in terms of achieving scale economies, as documented by, for example, Harris (1984), and by Wonnacott and Wonnacott (1967, 1982).

3 See Rugman (1980).

4 Glejser *et al.* (1980).

5 In principle, an alternative policy would be to stimulate the merger of firms or to set up public agencies coordinating their activities. The former measure, however, is unlikely to be successful as smaller entrepreneurial firms cannot be turned into large corporations without creating internal inefficiencies. The problem associated with the latter support programme is that a single agency will be faced with a heterogeneous set of demands emanating from the different small firms. The specialized nature of required marketing and distribution efforts to be developed for each individual firm are likely to make the activities of any coordinating agency completely ineffective, unless of course its role is restricted to that of a 'facilitator' of contacts between the firms and foreign customers, for example through international trade fairs.

6 Basic studies on the issue of penetration include Spence (1977) and Dixit (1980). The possible implications for government support programmes are discussed in Brander (1987b).

7 See, for example, Spence (1984).

8 Rugman and McIlveen (1985).

9 See Phillips (1966) and Kamien and Schwartz (1982).
10 In a recent study on the theoretical foundations of an active industrial policy for small open economies, Harris has developed a number of specific recommendations to guide public policy makers in designing efficient interventionist policies. Unfortunately, as recognized by the author himself, Harris issues these suggestions without careful analysis of their political and bureaucratic feasibility. This feasibility obviously includes the implementation possibilities of policy choices. See Harris (1985).
11 Harris (1985).

Chapter 9   Industrial policy and global competition: Ontario's experience

1 Also, see Rugman and Verbeke (1987, 1988a and 1989).
2 See Rugman and McIlveen (1985).
3 See Ontario Premier's Council (1988–9).
4 See Rugman (1988c).
5 As discussed in Hornell and Vahlne (1986).
6 This has been demonstrated by D'Cruz and Fleck (1987), Rugman (1988c) and others.
7 For a discussion of the economic impact of all multinationals on the Canadian economy, see Rugman (1990).
8 As discussed in Rugman and Verbeke (1987).
9 As discussed in Rugman and Verbeke (1988b and 1989).
10 See Krugman (1986).
11 As discussed by the Board of Trade of Metropolitan Toronto (1989).
12 McMillan (1989).

Bibliography

Abegglen, James, C. and Stalk, George Jr. (1985), *Kaisha, the Japanese Company*, New York: Basic Books.

Baldwin, Robert E. (1985) *The Political Economy of U.S. Import Policy*, Cambridge, Mass.: MIT Press.

—— (1986) 'Trade policies in developed countries', in R. W. Jones (ed.) *International Trade: Surveys of Theory and Policy*, Amsterdam, New York: North Holland.

Baldwin, John and Gorecki, Paul (1986) *The Role of Scale in Canada–U.S. Productivity Differences in the Manufacturing Sector*, Toronto: University of Toronto Press.

Baranson, Jack (1985) 'Assessment of likely impact of a U.S.–Canada Free Trade Agreement upon the behavior of U.S. industrial subsidiaries in Canada', Toronto: Ministry of Industry, Trade and Technology, Province of Ontario.

Bartlett, Christopher A. (1986) 'Building and managing the transnational: the new organizational challenge', in M. E. Porter (ed.) *Competition in Global Industries*, Boston: Harvard Business School Press, pp. 367–404.

Bauer, Raymond A., de Sola, Ithiel and Dexter, Lewis A. (1972) *American Business and Public Policy: The Politics of Foreign Trade*, Chicago: Aldine Atherton.

Board of Trade of Metropolitan Toronto (1989) 'Response to the Report of the Premier's Council "Competing in the New Global Economy" ', mimeo, January.

Brander, James A. (1987a) 'Shaping comparative advantage: trade policy, industrial policy and economic performance', in Richard G. Lipsey and Wendy Dobson (eds) *Shaping Comparative Advantage*, Toronto: C. D. Howe Institute, pp. 1–56.

—— (1987b) 'Rationales for strategic trade and industrial policy', in Paul R. Krugman (ed.) *Strategic Trade Policy and the New International Economics*, Boston: MIT Press, pp. 1–21.

Brander, James A. and Spencer, Barbara J. (1985) 'Export subsidies and international market share rivalry', *Journal of International Economics* 18: 83–100.

150

Breton, Albert (1974) *The Economic Theory of Representative Government*, Chicago: Aldine.

Brock, William A. and Magee, Stephen P. (1978) 'The economics of special interest politics: the case of the tariff', *American Economic Review* 68, 2 (May): 246–50.

Brown, C. V. and Jackson, P. M. (1982) *Public Sector Economies*, Oxford: Martin Robertson.

Buchanan, James M. and Tullock, Gordon, (1962) *The Calculus of Consent*, Ann Arbor: University of Michigan Press.

Burgess, David F. (1985) 'The impact of trade liberalization on foreign direct investment flows', in J. Whalley and R. Hill (eds) *Canada–United States Free Trade* Vol. II, Toronto: University of Toronto Press, pp. 193–200.

—— (1986) 'Implications of a U.S.–Canadian trade agreement for factor flows and plant locations', mimeo.

Calingaert, Michael (1988) *The 1992 Challenge From Europe: Development of the European Community's Internal Market*, Washington, DC: National Planning Association.

Canada, MSS (1988) *Canada's International Investment Position – 1985*, Statistics Canada No. 67–202, Ottawa: Ministry of Supply and Services.

Canada, DEA (1988) *The Canada–U.S. Free Trade Agreement*, Ottawa: Department of External Affairs.

Caves, Richard E. (1976) 'Economic models of political choice: Canada's tariff structure', *Canadian Journal of Economics* 9, 2 (May): 278–300.

—— (1982) *Multinational Enterprise and Economic Analysis*, New York: Cambridge University Press.

Cecchini, Paolo (1988) *The European Challenge 1992: The Benefits of a Single Market*, Aldershot: Wildwood House.

CFIB (1988) 'Submission to the Ontario standing committee on finance and economic affairs', Toronto, 8 March, Canadian Federation of Independent Business.

CIAR (1988) *Innovation and Canada's Prosperity: The Transforming of Science, Engineering and Technology*, Toronto, Canadian Institute for Advanced Research.

Cline, William R. (1989) 'Macro-economic influences on trade policy', *American Economic Review*, 79, 2: 123–7.

Commission of the European Communities (1988) 'The Economics of 1992', *European Economy* 35 (March): 1–222.

Coopers and Lybrand (1988) *Implications for Free Trade and Canadian Corporate Strategies*, Ottawa: Department of Finance.

Crookell, Harold (1987) 'Managing Canadian subsidiaries in a free trade environment', *Sloan Management Review* (Fall): 71–6.

Curzon, Gerard (1989) 'Ten reasons to fear Fortress Europe', mimeo, Geneva: Graduate Institute of International Studies, June.

Curzon, G. and Curzon, V. (1987) 'Follies in European trade relations with Japan', *The World Economy* 10, 2 (June): 155–76.

Bibliography

Daly, Donald and MacCharles, Donald (1986) *Canadian Manufactured Exports: Constraints and Opportunities*, Halifax, Nova Scotia: The Institute for Research on Public Policy.

D'Cruz, Joseph (1986) 'Strategic management of subsidiaries', in Hamid Etemad and Louise Seguin Dulude (eds) *Managing the Multinational Subsidiary*, London: Croom Helm, pp. 75–89.

D'Cruz, Joseph and Fleck, James (1988) *Yankee Canadians in the Global Economy*, London, Ontario: National Centre for Management Research and Development, University of Western Ontario.

Destler, I. M. (1986) *American Trade Politics: System Under Stress*, Washington, DC: Institute for International Economics.

Dixit, Avinash (1980) 'The role of investment in entry deterrence', *Economic Journal* 90: 95–106.

Doz, Yves L. (1986a) *Strategic Management in Multinational Companies*, Oxford: Pergamon Press.

Doz, Yves L. (1986b) 'Government policies and global industries', in Michael E. Porter (ed.) *Competition in Global Industries*, Cambridge, Mass.: Harvard Business School Press.

Dunning, John and Rugman, Alan M. (1985) 'The contribution of Hymer's dissertation to the theory of foreign direct investment', *American Economic Review* 75, 2 (May): 228–32.

Economic Council of Canada (1988) *Managing Adjustment: Policies for Trade Sensitive Industries*, Ottawa: Economic Council of Canada.

—— (1988) *Venturing Forth: an Assessment of the Canada–U.S. Trade Agreement*, Ottawa.

Emerson, Michael, Arijean, Michel, Catinat, Michel, Goybet, Phillippe and Jacquemin, Alexis (1988) *The Economics of 1992: The E.C. Commission's Assessment of the Economic Effects of Completing the Internal Market* (1983) New York: Oxford University Press.

Ethier, Wilfred (1983) *Modern International Economics*, New York: Norton.

Farrow, Maureen and Rugman, Alan M. (eds) (1988) *Business Strategies and Free Trade*, Toronto: C.D. Howe Institute.

Finger, J. M. (1981) 'The industry–country incidence of "less than fair value" cases in U.S. import trade', *Quarterly Review of Economics and Business* 25, 2 (Summer).

Finger, J. M. and Nogues, Julio (1987) 'International control of subsidies and countervailing duties', *The World Bank Economic Review* 1, 4: 707–25.

Finger, J. M., Hall, H. Keith and Nelson, Douglas (1982) 'The political economy of administered protection', *American Economic Review* 72, 3 (June): 452–6.

Friberg, Erik G. (1989) '1992: moves Europeans are making', *Harvard Business Review* 67, 3 (May–June): 85–9.

GATT (1980–8) *Basic Instruments and Selected Documents (BISD)*, Supplements 27–35, General Agreement on Tariffs and Trades.

GATT (1988) *Report of the Committee on Subsidies and Countervailing Measures*, General Agreement on Tariffs and Trades (photocopy).

Glejser, H. A., Jacquemin, A. and Petit, J. (1980) 'Exports in an imperfect competition framework: an analysis of 1446 exporters', *Quarterly Journal of Economics* 20: 508–24.

Gove, Tom (1988) 'Proctor and Gamble Corporate Statement on the Canada–U.S. Free Trade Agreement', by the Manager of Management Systems and Distribution.

Grant, George (1965) *Lament for a Nation*, Toronto: McClelland and Stewart.

Harris, Richard G. (1984) 'Applied general equilibrium analysis of small open economies with scale economies and implement competition', *American Economic Review* 74: 1016–32.

—— (1985) *Trade, Industrial Policy and International Competition*, University of Toronto Press: Toronto.

Harris, Richard G. and Cox, David, (1984) *Trade, Industrial Policy and Canadian Manufacturing*, Toronto: Ontario Economic Council.

Hornell, Eric and Vahlne, Jan-Erik (1986) *Multinationals: The Swedish Case*, London: Croom Helm.

Hosoya, C. (1979) 'Relations between the European communities and Japan', *Journal of Common Market Studies* 18: 168–9.

Hufbauer, Gary C. and Erb, Joanna (1985) *Subsidies in International Trade*, Cambridge, Mass.: MIT Press.

Hufbauer, Gary C. and Rosen, Howard F. (1986) *Trade Policy for Troubled Industries*, Washington, DC: Institute for International Economics, March.

Hufbauer, Gary C., Berliner, Diane T. and Elliott, Kimberly Ann (1986) *Trade Protection in the United States: 31 Case Studies*, Washington, DC: Institute for International Economics.

Innis, Harold (1956) *The Fur Trade in Canada: An Introduction to Canadian Economic History*, Toronto: University of Toronto Press.

Kamien, M. I. and Schwartz, N. L. (1982) *Market Structure and Innovation*, Cambridge, Mass.: Cambridge University Press.

Kapteijn, P. J. G. and Verloren Van Themaat, P. (1980) *Inleiding tot Het Recht van de Europese Gemeenschappen* (Deventer).

Kostecki, M. (1987) 'Export-restraint announcements and trade liberalization', *The World Economy* 10, 4 December: 425–53.

Krueger, Anne (1986) 'Trade policies in developing countries', in Ronald W. Jones (ed.) *International Trade: Surveys of Theory and Policy*, Amsterdam: North Holland.

Krugman, Paul (ed.) (1986) *Strategic Trade Policy and the New International Economics*, Cambridge, Mass.: MIT Press.

Kwoka, J. E. Jr. (1984) 'Market power and market change in the U.S. automobile industry', *Journal of Industrial Economics* 32, 4 (June).

Kymlicka, B. B. (1987) 'Steel goes to Washington: lessons in lobbying', *Business Quarterly* 52, 2 (Fall): 98–100.

Lavergne, Real P. (1981) 'The political economy of U.S. tariffs', Ph. D. Dissertation, University of Toronto.

Lawrence, Robert Z. (1989) 'Protection: is there a better way?', *American Economic Review* 74, 2 (May): 118–22.

Bibliography

Lawrence, Robert Z. and Litan, Robert E. (1987) 'Why protectionism doesn't pay', *Harvard Business Review* 87, 3 (May–June): 60–7.

Laxer, James (1987) *Decline of the Superpowers*, Toronto: Lorimer.

Leibenstein, Harvey (1976) *Beyond Economic Man*, Cambridge, Mass.: Harvard University Press.

Le Monde (1988) 'Les enterprises européennes face a un marche unique', 15 October.

Lenway, Stefanie A. (1983) 'The impact of American business on international trade policy', in Lee E. Preston (ed.) *Research in Corporate Social Performance and Policy* Vol. 5, Greenwich, Conn.: JAI Press, pp. 27–58.

——— (1985) *The Politics of U.S. International Trade*, Boston: Pitman.

Lindblom, Charles E. (1977) *Politics and Markets: The World's Political–Economic Systems*, New York: Basic Books.

Lindsay, Cotton (1976) 'A theory of government enterprise', *Journal of Political Economy* 84, 5 (October): 1067–78.

Lipsey, Richard and Dobson, Wendy (eds) (1987) *Shaping Comparative Advantage*, Toronto: C. D. Howe Institute.

Lipsey, Richard G. and York, Robert C. (1988) *Evaluating the Free Trade Deal: A Guided Tour Through the Canada–U.S. Agreement*, Toronto: C. D. Howe Institute.

Litvak, Isaiah A. (1986) 'Freer trade with the United States: the conflicting views of Canadian business', *Business Quarterly* 51, 1 (Spring) 22–32.

London Business School (1989) *1992: Myths and Realities*, London: Centre for Business Strategy, London Business School.

MacCharles, Donald (1987) *Trade Among Multinationals: Intra-Industry Trade and National Competitiveness*, London: Croom Helm.

Mayhew, D. (1974) *Congress: The Electoral Connection*, New Haven: Yale University Press.

McCraw, Thomas K. (1986a) 'From partners to competitors: an overview of the period since World War II', in Thomas K. McCraw (ed.) *America vs. Japan*, Boston, Mass.: Harvard Business School Press, pp. 1–34.

McCraw, Thomas K. (ed.) (1986b) *America vs Japan*, Boston, Mass: Harvard Business School Press.

McCraw, Thomas K. and O'Brien, Patricia A. (1986) 'Production and distribution: competition policy and industry structure', in Thomas K. McCraw (ed.) *America vs. Japan*, Boston, Mass.: Harvard Business School Press, pp. 77–116.

McMillan, Charles J. (1989) *Investing in Tomorrow: Japan's Science and Technology Organization and Strategies*, Ottawa: Canada–Japan Trade Council.

Messerlin, Patrick A. (1989) 'The EC antidumping regulations: a first economic appraisal, 1980–85', *Weltwirtschaftliches Archiv* (forthcoming).

Milner, Helen (1987) 'Resisting the protectionist temptation: industry and the United States during the 1970s', *International Organization* 41, 4 (Autumn): 639–65.

Morici, Peter (1984) *The Global Competitive Struggle: Challenge to the United States and Canada*, Toronto: C. D. Howe Institute.

Mueller, Dennis (1979) *Public Choice*, Cambridge: Cambridge University Press.

Newall, Ted (1988) 'Stepping out from behind the tariff wall', in Earle Gray (ed.) *Free Trade: Free Canada*, Woodville: Canadian Speeches, pp. 53–6.

Niskanen, W. (1971) *Bureaucracy and Representative Government*, Chicago: Aldine Atherton.

Norman, Christopher (1986) 'New trends in anti-dumping practice in Brussels', *The World Economy* 9, 1 (March).

OECD (1985) *Costs and Benefits of Protection*, Paris: OECD.

Ohmae, Kenichi (1985) *Triad Power: The Coming Shape of Global Competition*, New York: The Free Press.

—— (1987) *Beyond National Borders*, Homewood, Ill.: Dow Jones–Irwin.

Olson, Mancur (1965) *The Logic of Collective Action: Public Goods and the Theory of Groups*, Cambridge, Mass.: Harvard University Press.

Ontario Premier's Council (1988–9) *Competing in the New Global Economy* (3 vols), Toronto: Queen's Printer of Ontario.

Ouchi, William G. (1984) *The M-Form Society*, Reading, Mass.: Addison-Wesley.

Pearce, J. and Sutton, J. (1986) *Protection and Industrial Policy in Europe*, London: Routledge and Kegan Paul.

Phillips, A. (1966) 'Patents, potential competition and technical progress', *American Economic Review* 56: 301–10.

Porter, Michael E. (1980) *Competitive Strategy: Techniques for Analyzing Industries and Competitors*, New York: The Free Press Macmillan.

—— (1985) *Competitive Advantage: Creating and Sustaining Superior Economic Performance*, New York: The Free Press Macmillan.

—— (ed.) (1986) *Competition in Global Industries*, Cambridge, Mass.: Harvard Business School Press.

Ray, Edward J. (1981) 'The determinants of tariff and non-tariff trade restrictions in the United States', *Journal of Political Economy* 89:1 (February): 105–21.

Rugman, Alan M. (1980) *Multinationals in Canada: theory, performance and economic impact*, Boston: Martinus Nijhoff.

—— (1981) *Inside the Multinationals: The Economics of Internal Markets*, London: Croom Helm; New York: Columbia University Press.

—— (1985) 'A Canadian strategy for international competitiveness', *Business Quarterly* 50, 3 (Fall): 18–21.

____ (1986a) 'National strategies for international competitiveness', in Proceedings of the 4th International Congress of the North American Economics and Finance Association, *Issues in North American Trade and Finance*, Montreal, pp. 315–26.

____ (1986b) 'U.S. Protectionism and Canadian Trade Policy', *Journal of World Trade Law* 20, 4 (July–August): 363–80.

____ (1987a) 'Living with free trade: how multinationals will adjust to trade liberalization', *Business Quarterly* 52, 2 (Fall) 85–90.

____ (1987b) *Outward Bound: Canadian Direct Investment in the United States*, Toronto: C. D. Howe Institute for the Canadian–American Committee.

____ (1988a) 'A Canadian perspective on U.S. administered protection and the Free Trade Agreement', *Maine Law Review* (September): 305–24.

____ (1988b) 'Multinational enterprises and strategies for international competitiveness', in Richard W. Farmer and Elton G. McGown (eds) *Advances in International Comparative Management*, Vol. 3, Greenwich, Conn.: JAI Press, pp. 47–58.

____ (1988c) 'The Free Trade Agreement and the global economy', *Business Quarterly* 53, 1 (Summer): 13–20.

____ (1988d) 'The multinational enterprise', in Ingo Walter and Tracy Murray (eds), *Handbook of International Management*, New York: Wiley, pp. 1–15.

____ (1988e) *Trade Liberalization and International Investment*, Ottawa: Economic Council of Canada, April.

____ (1988f) 'Why business supports free trade', in John Crispo (ed.) *Free Trade: The Real Story*, Toronto: Gage Education Publishing Company, 95–104.

____ (1990) *Multinationals and Canada–United States Free Trade*, Columbia: University of South Carolina Press.

Rugman, Alan M. and Anderson, Andrew, (1987a) *Administered Protection in America*, New York: Methuen; London: Croom Helm.

____ (1987b) 'A fishy business: the abuse of American trade law in the Atlantic groundfish case of 1985–1986', *Canadian Public Policy* XIII, 2 (June): 152–64.

____ (1989) 'How to make the Free Trade Agreement work: implementing the dispute settlement measures and the subsidies code', Toronto: C. D. Howe *Trade Monitor* no. X, July.

Rugman, Alan M. and McIlveen, John (1985) *Megafirms: Strategies for Canada's Multinationals*, Toronto: Methuen.

Rugman, Alan M. and Porteous, Samuel, (1988) 'The softwood lumber decision of 1986: broadening the nature of U.S. administered protection', *Review of International Business Law* 2, 1 (April) 35–58.

Rugman, Alan M. and Verbeke, Alain (1987) 'Trade policy for the Asia–Pacific region: a U.S.–Japan comparison', *Journal of Business Administration* 17, 1–2: 89–107.

____ (1988a) 'Strategic responses to free trade', in Maureen Farrow and

Alan M. Rugman (eds) *Business Strategies and Free Trade*, Toronto: C. D. Howe Institute, 13–30.

—— (1988b) 'Shelter, trade policy and strategies for multinational enterprises', Discussion Paper no. 10, Toronto: Ontario Centre for International Business, University of Toronto.

—— (1989) 'Trade policy and global corporate strategy', *Journal of Global Marketing* 2, 3 (Spring): 1–17.

Rugman, Alan M. and Warner, Mark (1988) *Corporate Responses to Free Trade: Strategies for Canada's Multinationals*, National Centre for Management Research and Development Discussion Paper 88–10 (May).

Rugman, Alan M., Lecraw, Donald and Booth, Laurence (1985) *International Business: Firm and Environment*, New York: McGraw Hill.

Safarian, Edward (1985) 'The relationship between trade agreements and international direct investment', in W. Conklin and T. J. Courchene (eds) *Canadian Trade at a Crossroads: Options for New International Agreements*, Toronto: Ontario Economic Council, pp. 206–21.

Spence, A. Michael (1977) 'Entry investment and oligopolistic pricing', *Bell Journal of Economics* 8: 534–44.

—— (1984) 'Cost reduction, competition and industry performance', *Econometrica* 52: 101–21.

Statistics Canada (various years) Publication no. 61–210, *Corporations and Labour Unions Return Act* (CALURA), Part I.

Thorne, Ernst and Whinney (1988) *Canada–U.S. Free Trade Agreement: A Survey of North American Business Leaders*, Toronto.

Tullock, Gordon (1965) *The Politics of Bureaucracy*, Washington, DC: Public Affairs Press.

Tyson, Laura (1987) 'Creating advantage: an industrial policy perspective', in Lipsey and Dobson (eds) *Shaping Comparative Advantage*, Toronto: C. D. Howe Institute, pp. 65–82.

Vandermerwe, Sandra (1989) 'Strategies for a pan-European market', *Long Range Planning* 22, 3: 45–53.

Williamson, Oliver E. (1975) *Markets and Hierarchies: Analysis and Antitrust Implications*, New York: The Free Press Macmillan.

—— (1985) *The Economic Institutions of Capitalism*, New York: The Free Press Macmillan.

Winham, Gilbert (1987) *International Trade and the Tokyo Round Negotiation*, Princeton, NJ: Princeton University Press.

Wonnacott, Paul (1987) *The United States and Canada: The Quest for Free Trade*, Washington, DC: The Institute for International Economics.

Wonnacott, Paul and Wonnacott, R. J. (1967) *Free Trade Between the United States and Canada: The Potential Economic Effects*, Cambridge, Mass: Harvard University Press.

—— (1982) 'Free trade between the United States and Canada: fifteen years later', *Canadian Public Policy* 8, Special Supplement, October.

Bibliography

World Bank (1988) *World Development Report 1988*, Washington, DC: World Bank.

Yoffie, David B. (1986) 'Protecting world markets', in Thomas K. McCraw (ed.) *America vs. Japan*, Boston, Mass.: Harvard Business School Press, pp. 35–76.

Name index

Company index

161

Company index

Subject index